FOCUSED for RUGBY

Adam R. Nicholls
Jon Callard

Human Kinetics

Library of Congress Cataloging-in-Publication Data

Nicholls, Adam R.
  Focused for rugby / Adam Nicholls, Jon Callard.
    p. cm.
  ISBN 978-1-4504-0212-5 (soft cover) -- ISBN 1-4504-0212-7 (soft cover) 1.
Rugby football--Psychological aspects. 2. Rugby football--Training. I.
Callard, Jon, 1966- II. Title.
  GV945.85.P75N54 2012
  796.333'8--dc23
                                  2011047312

ISBN-10: 1-4504-0212-7 (print)
ISBN-13: 978-1-4504-0212-5 (print)

The web addresses cited in this text were current as of December 2011, unless otherwise noted.

Acquisitions Editor: Peter Murphy; **Developmental Editor:** Anne Hall; **Assistant Editor:** Tyler Wolpert; **Copyeditor:** Bob Replinger; **Permissions Manager:** Martha Gullo; **Graphic Designer:** Bob Reuther; **Graphic Artist:** Julie L. Denzer; **Cover Designer:** Keith Blomberg; **Photographer (cover):** Peter Muhly/AFP/Getty Images; **Photographer (interior):** Neil Bernstein, unless otherwise noted; **Photo Asset Manager:** Laura Fitch; **Visual Production Assistant:** Joyce Brumfield; **Photo Production Manager:** Jason Allen; **Art Manager:** Kelly Hendren; **Associate Art Manager:** Alan L. Wilborn; **Illustrations:** © Human Kinetics, unless otherwise noted; **Printer:** United Graphics

Human Kinetics books are available at special discounts for bulk purchase. Special editions or book excerpts can also be created to specification. For details, contact the Special Sales Manager at Human Kinetics.

Printed in the United States of America   10 9 8 7 6 5 4 3 2 1

The paper in this book is certified under a sustainable forestry program.

Human Kinetics
Website: www.HumanKinetics.com

United States: Human Kinetics
P.O. Box 5076
Champaign, IL 61825-5076
800-747-4457
e-mail: humank@hkusa.com

Canada: Human Kinetics
475 Devonshire Road Unit 100
Windsor, ON N8Y 2L5
800-465-7301 (in Canada only)
e-mail: info@hkcanada.com

Europe: Human Kinetics
107 Bradford Road
Stanningley
Leeds LS28 6AT, United Kingdom
+44 (0) 113 255 5665
e-mail: hk@hkeurope.com

Australia: Human Kinetics
57A Price Avenue
Lower Mitcham, South Australia 5062
08 8372 0999
e-mail: info@hkaustralia.com

New Zealand: Human Kinetics
P.O. Box 80
Torrens Park, South Australia 5062
0800 222 062
e-mail: info@hknewzealand.com

E5302

To my parents, George and Christine, thank you
for all the support you have given me over the years.
—Adam

To my three lovely daughters, Georgia, Francesca, and Alexa,
who put up with me, and to my wife, Gail, without whose support
I would not be allowed to pursue my dreams in the sport of rugby.
—Jon

Contents

Foreword

I am delighted to have been asked to contribute the foreword for *Focused for Rugby*. I have known Jon Callard for more than 20 years, both as a player I coached and as a coach I worked alongside. One of Jon's great strengths was his goal-kicking ability, a skill in which players stand alone in the big arena with all the attendant pressures that it can bring. Performing this technique successfully at all levels requires real mental clarity.

Focused for Rugby is an interactive book for both players and coaches, whatever their age and experience. This book also sets out all the information simply and explains why the mental side of the game is so important. I have to put my hand on my heart and say that I am not a massive fan of the term *sport psychology*, but I am a fervent believer in the importance of developing the mental skills that enable players to focus solely on the task at hand whilst actions and thoughts fight to interfere with successful execution of the job. Rugby has changed dramatically over the last 20 years, but I suspect that for the majority of coaches and players, the mental side of the game—the glue that holds together the technical, physical, and tactical sides of the game under the most hostile pressure—is the least understood and practised, which is why *Focused for Rugby* is very much needed!

Many coaches and players equate mental toughness with physical toughness. Nothing could be further from the truth. We have all witnessed the macho player doing the most ridiculously off-task things in the heat of battle, to the detriment of his companions and the outcome of a game. The mental side of the game demands as much regular practice as all the other elements of high-level performance. It requires much more than just dabbling now and again. The skill involves honing a mindset of great clarity under intense scrutiny to enable consistent success and not in a haphazard fashion. This skill is emphasised in *Focused for Rugby* as you are encouraged to practice psychological skills and monitor your own progress.

In my mind, I am perfectly clear about one thing. A coach and a group of players who use the techniques that you will read about in *Focused for Rugby* will be on the road to success in the sport.

Enjoy reading *Focused for Rugby*, and enjoy the success! Good luck.

—Brian Ashton, MBE

Introduction

The purpose of this introduction is to explain what sport psychology is, discuss the myths surrounding it, the potential benefits of sport psychology in rugby, and how to use this book effectively.

Psychology is concerned with the mind and the reasons why people think and act the way that they do. *Sport psychology* is concerned with the way that athletes think and behave whilst playing sport. The two primary goals of sport psychology are to (*a*) ensure the well-being of athletes whilst playing sport and (*b*) enhance their performance.

Many athletes, coaches, and sport commentators seem to misunderstand sport psychology, which often gives this discipline a negative reputation. This stigma is partly fueled by unqualified individuals who practise as sport psychologists and give the players whom they work with false expectations. Seeing a sport psychologist is not like having a magic wand waved in front of you. Sport psychologists don't have any special powers! Reading this book will not transform you or your performance within seconds. This book offers techniques that, when practiced, will enable you to fulfil your potential during training and matches, in addition to enhancing your emotional well-being.

Some players or coaches view seeing a sport psychologist as a weakness. Yet rugby players spend many hours working on physical, technical, and tactical aspects of their game, so why should they not work on the mental side, too? After all, we have all seen players who perform very well in training but not in matches. So what stops a player from being good in training but not in matches? Physically, the athlete is the same player, so it could be the mental side of his or her game. Learning sport psychology skills will enable players to perform during the heat of the battle and even excel during matches.

Callard the PLAYER

We had just been awarded the penalty, just in the Scotland half. I knew the game was nearing the end, and I thought it could be the last chance to win it. I started to focus on the process and not the outcome. I had previously missed two kicks, and I knew why these had missed. I focused on getting a sweet swing, controlling the sequence, and a having a clear understanding of where I was aiming. I took my paces back from the ball, steadied myself, took a deep breath to calm myself down, centred my body, and focused on not being quick and striking the sweet spot. . . .The flags were raised, England's hopes of grand slam lived on, and we won the match 15-14.

Negative thoughts, fear of failure, and concerns about what other players or coaches think are some of the factors that stop rugby players from performing at their best. The aim of this book is to teach you psychological techniques that you can use whilst playing, training, or preparing to play and train to help you maintain emotional well-being and perform at your best. In short, the *benefits* of sport psychology will be discussed.

This book has been written to give players and coaches of all levels an understanding and practical advice about how to do sport psychology yourself or, if you are a coach, to teach your players psychological techniques. The book is structured so that you do not have to read each chapter. You can look at the contents page and decide which chapters are most appropriate for you. For instance, if you think that you do not cope as well with stress as you could during matches, chapter 5 will be useful to you. If you struggle to control your temper, chapter 10 may be an interesting chapter for you to read. Additionally, blank training table templates dispersed throughout the book can be found at http://tinyurl.com/7cft58w.

As we said previously, sport psychology is not magic. We make no guarantees about the effects of this book on your performance. We do not claim that reading this book will improve your performance by 10 percent. But we do offer techniques and ideas that you can use based on our backgrounds of research, consultancy, playing, and coaching. You may even find ways of adapting the techniques that we have suggested, which is fine.

We hope that you find *Focused for Rugby* informative and practical, and we wish you every success in using some of the techniques that we have suggested.

CHAPTER 1

Goal Setting

I had come to a turning point in my career. I was not going to be offered a new contract but still wanted to carry on playing professionally. I set myself some goals relating to my strength and conditioning and technical components of my game in order to improve and thus secure my ultimate goal—securing another contract with a different club. This really helped me get that next contract.

Peter, professional rugby union player

What Are Goals?

A goal is something that people are trying to achieve, such as being selected for a particular team, improving their tackling, or improving their kicking percentage.

Why is it important to set goals? Locke and Latham (1990), two prominent researchers in sport psychology, found that sport performers should set goals to

- ensure that they remain persistent in the face of either failure or adversity because they have something to strive for,
- focus their attention and direct their energy on what they want to achieve,
- help them maintain a consistently high level of effort and intensity through continual striving for goal attainment, and
- encourage them to develop new problem-solving strategies when setting new goals.

Setting Goals Over a Prolonged Time Frame

Goals can be short term, medium term, or long term. A short-term goal relates to attaining something that will happen shortly after a goal is set, such as winning your next match the following day or the following week. A medium-term goal refers to goals set to occur over a time of months to a season, such as wanting to make 20 appearances for a particular team during a season. Finally, long-term goals are goals that are set for times longer than a season. For instance, a long-term goal of a 14-year-old rugby player might be to represent his or her country or to attain a professional contract.

All rugby players should set a variety of short-term, medium-term, and long-term goals. First, long-term goals are crucial for providing you with a sense of purpose and making the sacrifices that you will inevitably have to make seem worthwhile. Medium-term and short-term goals make longer-term goals seem more achievable because by repeatedly achieving your short-term and medium-term goals, you will eventually succeed in achieving your long-term goals.

Different Types of Goals

You can set three types of goals: (1) outcome goals, (2) performance goals, and (3) process goals. These goals can be set over different times, such as the short, medium, or long term. The important element of these goals is not the time in which they are set over, but the content of the goals.

1. Outcome goals. Outcome goals are concerned with the result or outcome of a particular match or competition. For example, a coach could set a goal of finishing in the top three of a league or winning a particular match. Although these goals are important, because success in sport is often determined by winning or losing, outcome goals are only partially controllable by a team or individual. Success in achieving these goals depends on many others, such as opponents, teammates, and officials. For instance, the team who finishes fourth in the league may have performed to their maximum potential and would never have been good enough to win the league. The team who lost a match may have done so only because of poor officiating. Caution is warranted in setting only outcome goals, because they can result in decreased motivation. Outcome goals can be used in combination with performance and process goals.

2. Performance goals. Performance goals are directly related to standards of performance that a rugby player wants to achieve, such as to improve the percentage of successful goal kicks by 10 percent from 55 percent to 65 percent, to improve sprint times over 30 metres by 0.4 of a second from 4.8 seconds to 4.4 seconds, or to improve the percentage of lineout throws by 5 percent from 80 percent to 85 percent. When setting these goals you are competing against yourself and trying to better yourself.

3. Process goals. Process goals are targets focused on specific actions within a movement. For example, a lineout jumper may have poor knee flex before being lifted at the lineout and a goal for this player could be to improve his or her knee flex for extra spring in the lineout jump. A process goal for a goal kicker could be to follow through with his or her leg. Essentially, process goals enable you to improve your performance by concentrating on the specific elements of the required movement.

Callard the COACH

A team I once coached was in a particularly daunting situation. We were 12 points adrift from our nearest rivals at the foot of the Premiership. We were a side of exceptionally hard-working individuals, but the atmosphere within the team was one of despair because of our league position.

If we had any chance of survival, we needed to change our goals. Staying up was obviously the main goal, but it was blinding us in our pursuit. We needed greater clarity for the task ahead and greater understanding about the processes that we needed to follow to achieve our goal and stay in the Premiership. Outcome goals had worked initially, but now we needed to assess and evaluate our performance goals. These were the real tangibles that everyone could live and breathe every day.

We called our position "Bad debt." We accepted that we couldn't just forget about it, nor could we pay it off in one go. We realised what the issues were and how we were going to address them. We set several goals:

1. We wanted to make more effective tackles. Effective tackles were classified as those that stopped the opposition, turned the ball over, or were awarded a penalty for our team.

2. We wanted to eliminate 90 percent of handling errors in training, and, as coaches, we wanted to support the lines that the players made in training.

3. We had a clear points structure, in that we wanted every visit within 35 metres of the opposition try line to be rewarded with points.

4. Finally, we wanted teammates to have more respect for each other. We encouraged players to do something that gained the respect of their teammates (e.g., turning up early for training, helping to clear the kit away, doing extra training, and encouraging others to do extra training).

Within three weeks of setting these new goals we got our rewards. We beat the top side at home and went on an unbeaten run to the end of the season. The performance goals that we established in the need of change had really worked. Premiership survival and a cup triumph was the result of our change in thinking!

Icon Sports Media

Setting goals, such as improving kicking skills, helps players like Australia's Quade Cooper focus on what they want to achieve.

Setting Effective Goals by Setting SMARTER Goals

A method of ensuring that your goals are effective is to set SMARTER goals. As such, goals should be specific, measurable, action-orientated, realistic, timed, and elastic. See table 1.1 about setting SMARTER goals.

Goal-Setting Styles

Scholars from the sport psychology literature (Burton & Naylor, 2002) suggested that athletes naturally set particular types of goals depending on their personality. The two types of goal-setting styles are (*a*) performance-orientated goal-setting styles and (*b*) success-orientated goal setting styles.

   1. Performance-orientated goal setting styles. Athletes with a performance-orientated approach to setting goals are more likely to set goals that are related to self-improvement (e.g., I want to improve my passing technique) rather than to demonstrating their superior ability over teammates (e.g., I want to be able to pass better than the other scrum-half). Players with performance-orientated approaches focus on improving their own game and view most opportunities as a chance to improve their game. As such, players with this style of goal setting are likely to set challenging and difficult goals, even at the risk of making mistakes,

TABLE 1.1   SMARTER Goals in Rugby

Goal principle	Setting effective goals
Specific	Goals should be clear and straightforward and include exactly what you want to happen (e.g., achieve professional contract). Research suggests that specific goals lead to better performance than goals such as "I will do my best."
Measurable	Goals that are measurable can result in enhanced motivation. You need to assess your current level of ability in a goal that you want to set and work from there. So, if you currently make on average 14 tackles per game, a goal might be to increase this number to 16 tackles per game over the next month. Remember, if you can't measure it, you can't manage it!
Action orientated	When you set your goals, you also need to consider how you are going to reach your overall performance goals. Just setting a goal does not mean that you will be able to achieve it. Hard work is required.
Realistic	Goals need to be realistic, but they also need to have an element of challenge. That is, if you work really hard on various elements of your game, you should be able to achieve your goals. If you set goals that you have no chance of achieving, you may experience a sharp decline in motivation and an increase in anxiety. Alternatively, if you set goals that are too easy, you may experience boredom. One way of ensuring that your goals are realistic is to speak to someone who knows your game, such as a coach or teammate.
Timed	Goals should be set within specific time frames. The time frame can vary dramatically from a goal set for the end of a particular day to a career goal that may occur 10 years after you first set it, such as representing your country at rugby. The crucial component is that goals should be timed so that you know when you want to achieve a specific goal.
Elastic	Allow for some flexibility in your goals. Instead of setting performance goals to exact percentages, set a percentage range. For instance, you might have started 14 games last season, so you could set a goal of starting 16 to 20 games this season instead of having a goal of starting 18 games. By having this flexibility, you will still feel motivated if you don't manage to start 18 games.
Repeatability	After you have achieved your goals, aim to repeat them again or set even higher goals. For instance, a team goal may be to win the league. After you do this, aim to win the league again by a higher point margin.

because their primary aim is to improve as players. Therefore, players who tend to set these types of goals are comfortable playing against superior opponents, because they judge success on their own improvement.

2. Success-orientated goal-setting styles. Players with a success-orientated goal-setting style focus on setting goals that are based on social comparisons between teammates or opposition players in addition to the outcome of matches. Players with this goal-setting style avoid setting challenging goals if they think that they risk suffering public humiliation by making lots of mistakes. Instead, they set moderately challenging goals that they are confident they can attain.

TASK Considering Goals That You Have Set for Yourself in the Past

Are they related to your own standards of performance, or are they related to comparisons between yourself and teammates or opponents?

The type of goals that you set is also likely to influence how much effort you put into your performance. For instance, the effort put in by players with a success-oriented goal setting style is likely to fluctuate depending on task difficulty (e.g., quality of opposition). When the quality of the opposition is moderately difficult these players will put in lots of effort to reach their goals, but they will expend only as little effort as necessary when the quality of the opposition is poor. When faced with incredibly tough opponents or a tough task, however, players who have success-orientated goals will exert high effort until they realise that they cannot outdo their opponents, and so they give up in some respects.

Conversely, players who set performance-orientated goals are likely to perform more consistently in different situations because these types of players are consistently trying to improve their own performance. They will therefore be continually striving to perform to their best and not worrying about how their opponents or their teammates are doing. As such, sport psychology researchers have suggested that athletes with performance-orientated goal styles are more likely to be successful than athletes with success-orientated goal styles because they maximise their chances of winning by performing consistently at their best.

Problems That May Prevent Effective Goal Setting

To prevent ineffective goal setting, do the following:

- Make sure that your goals motivate you. For this to happen, you need to be highly committed to achieving your goals. Without goal commitment, you will not make the sacrifices and do the hard work required for you to achieve the goals that you set.
- Don't set too many goals. If you set too many goals, your attention will be spread too broadly and you might not achieve any of your goals. Focus on one or two goals at a time. Achieve those goals and then set other goals.
- Change the goals that you have set if you think that they are either too easy or too hard to achieve. Don't be afraid to change your goals.
- Remember that setting goals will not automatically result in superior performance—you will need to put in the work.

- Make sure that the goals you set are specific and that you can measure whether you were successful in achieving them.

- Identify the barriers that may prevent you from achieving your goals. These could be other commitments that prevent you from doing the practice needed to reach your goals (e.g., education, work, or time restraints). If you cannot overcome the barriers, adjust your goals accordingly.

TASK   **Changing to a Performance-Orientated Goal Setting Style**

If you believe that you have a success-orientated goal-setting style (i.e., in the past you have set goals in relation to beating your teammates or opponents rather than improving your own performance), you can change to a performance-orientated goal-setting style with little difficulty, which will improve the consistency of your effort. To change your goal-setting style, do the following:

1. Focus on what you want to do and set goals that focus on learning and becoming more proficient in rugby-related activities. For example, you might want to set yourself a goal of improving your throw in the lineout or kicking at the goals. Focus on improvement and do not compare yourself with other players.

2. When setbacks occur, focus on new skills that you need to learn and practise them. If, for example you are dropped by your coach, you could focus on the skills that you need to work on to improve your performance such as your body alignment whilst tackling or the position of your hands when passing.

3. Embrace all challenges that you face and view matches as opportunities to learn, even if it means that you might make some mistakes. In a match your team might suffer a heavy defeat, but you might 'have learned new tactics from the team that you played against or the way that different players played against you, which you can incorporate into your own game through work in training.

Setting Your Own Rugby Goals

Now you should consider setting your own rugby goals. These goals should be personal to you because only goals that are personal and relevant to you will provide the motivation required to attain such goals. Before setting your own goals you should know what you want to achieve.

Stage 1: Know Where You Want to Go

To set your own goals, you need to have a clear picture of what it is you want to achieve. Before recording your personal goals, consider and then answer the questions in table 1.2 on page 8. Answer these questions honestly. Your answers are not for the benefit of your coaches, parents, or friends. They are for you.

TABLE 1.2	What You Want to Achieve in Rugby

Question	Your answer
What level do you want to play at (e.g., international, county, district, club).	
What do you think you will need to do to play at your desired level?	
What sacrifices are you prepared to make to achieve your goals?	
When do you think it will be possible to play at the level where you want to play?	
What could you do to ensure that you play at your desired level?	
How do you think achieving your goals will make you feel?	

From A. Nicholls and J. Callard, 2012, *Focused for rugby* (Champaign, IL: Human Kinetics).

Callard the PLAYER

When I still at school my goal was to play first-class rugby. I managed to play my first game for Newport when I was 17 and still at school. My goal was then to be a regular member of the first-team squad and to play for the first team on a regular basis. I spoke to the coaches to find out what I needed to do to be a first-team player. I then set myself goals of making positive contributions in every training session so that I could achieve my goal.

Stage 2: Set Your Own Goals

Now you have considered what it is that you want to do in rugby, you are ready to set your goals by completing your goal sheet. Table 1.3 is an example of a completed goal-setting sheet. Of course, you must answer the questions in relation to your own hopes and aspirations. Complete this goal-setting sheet for your

- long-term goals (e.g., career goals),
- midterm goals (e.g., goals for the season), and
- short-term goals (e.g., goals for each month).

You should complete these goal-setting sheets at the beginning of each season for the season ahead. You could also complete a goal-setting sheet at the beginning of each month to outline what you want to achieve and what barriers might prevent you from achieving them. The sheet has been designed with this in mind (see table 1.4 on page 10 for a blank template).

TABLE 1.3   Goal-Setting Sheet Example

Date: July 12
Goals for career, season, and month (circle as applicable).

LIST YOUR OUTCOME GOALS (E.G., RESULTS OF PARTICULAR MATCHES AND COMPETITION).	
Outcome goal	**Date to be achieved**
1. *Finish in top three of the league*	*June*
2. *Beat local rivals home and away*	*October and March*
3. *Win the cup*	*March*

LIST YOUR PERFORMANCE GOALS (E.G., KICKING PERFORMANCE, LINEOUT THROWING, NUMBER OF TACKLES) AND THE DATES WHEN YOU WANT TO ACHIEVE YOUR GOALS.	
Performance goals	**Date to be achieved**
1. *Improve goal-kicking performance from 63 percent to between 68 percent and 75 percent by practising four sessions per week.*	*April*
2. *Increase the number of successful tackles made from 8 to 10 to 15 per match. I will do this by working on my technique and by getting in better positions.*	*From the start of the season until the end of the season*
3. *Improve pass completion to between 85 and 90 percent of all passes by spending extra time after sessions working on passes.*	*April*

LIST YOUR PROCESS GOALS (E.G., FOCUS ON ACTIONS SUCH AS SHOULDER POSITION DURING TACKLING, PASSING ACTION, AND SO ON).	
Process goals	**Date to be achieved**
1. *Improve follow-through during kicking by improving drive and flexibility.*	*October until the rest of the season*
2. *Keep head down whilst kicking.*	*From the start of the season*
3. *Improve shoulder position in the tackle by spending extra time on tackling technique.*	*October*

LIST THE BARRIERS THAT MAY PREVENT YOU FROM ACHIEVING YOUR GOALS AND THE POSSIBLE SOLUTIONS, IF THERE ARE ANY.	
Barriers	**Possible solutions**
1. *University work*	*Plan what I need to do better and don't leave assignments until the last minute so that I have extra practice time.*
2. *Fitness*	*Make sure that I enter preseason much fitter by doing extra work.*
3. *Attitude*	*Remain positive throughout the whole season. Enjoy the extra practice.*

TABLE 1.4   Goal-Setting Sheet

Date: _____

Goals for career, season, and month (circle as applicable).

LIST YOUR OUTCOME GOALS (E.G., RESULTS OF PARTICULAR MATCHES AND COMPETITION).	
Outcome goal	Date to be achieved
1.	
2.	
3.	

LIST YOUR PERFORMANCE GOALS (E.G., KICKING PERFORMANCE, LINEOUT THROWING, NUMBER OF TACKLES) AND THE DATES WHEN YOU WANT TO ACHIEVE YOUR GOALS.	
Performance goals	Date to be achieved
1.	
2.	
3.	

LIST YOUR PROCESS GOALS (E.G., FOCUS ON ACTIONS SUCH AS SHOULDER POSITION DURING TACKLING, PASSING ACTION, AND SO ON).	
Process goals	Date to be achieved
1.	
2.	
3.	

LIST THE BARRIERS THAT MAY PREVENT YOU FROM ACHIEVING YOUR GOALS AND THE POSSIBLE SOLUTIONS, IF THERE ARE ANY.	
Barriers	Possible solutions
1.	
2.	
3.	

From A. Nicholls and J. Callard, 2012, *Focused for rugby* (Champaign, IL: Human Kinetics).

Stage 3: Review Your Goals

You should regularly review your goals and amend them as necessary. For example, the goals that you set might be too difficult to achieve in the time frame that you have set. If so, create a different goal. Alternatively, you might achieve a particular goal ahead of schedule. When this occurs, set yourself another goal.

Summary

- Effective goal setting can help you identify what you have to do to be where you want to be.
- Make sure that you have SMARTER goals.
- Set a range of short-term, medium-term, and long-term goals.
- Set a range of outcome, performance, and process goals.
- Remember to adjust your goals if required.
- Adopt a process-orientated goal-setting approach. Focus on your own improvements.
- Commit to your goals.
- Regularly revisit your goals and look over previous goals that you have set.
- Enjoy the feelings of achieving your goals!

CHAPTER 2

Performance Profiling

I knew that I needed to improve in order to make it into the first team, but I was not sure which areas of my game that I needed to improve. Profiling the most important attributes of a hooker helped me realise what I needed to do to reach those levels. It really gave me clarity, and the improvements I made helped me claim the first-team hooker jersey. I did not rest on my laurels and continually monitored my performance.

Matthew, ex-England U-20 international

What Is Performance Profiling?

Performance profiling involves three procedures. First, you list the characteristics that you think are the most important for success in rugby based on your playing position. Then you can list a range of qualities that the best players have in your position, which may include

- physical (e.g., strength, speed, fitness),
- technical (e.g., passing technique, scrummaging technique, kicking),
- tactical (e.g., reading of game, positional play), and
- psychological (e.g., ability to manage stress, mental toughness).

Second, you then select the most important characteristics and write down what that characteristic means to you. Finally, you rate your current ability for each quality you have listed on a scale of 1 to 10. The performance profile is a personalised tool, and two rugby players are unlikely to have the same profile.

What Are the Benefits of the Performance Profile?

Sport psychology researchers (e.g., Jones, 1993) have established several benefits of the performance profile:

1. Identifying the characteristics that help successful performance in rugby
2. Identifying your strengths and weaknesses
3. Increasing your understanding of your abilities and what is required to be successful in the position that you play
4. Identifying what you should work on to increase your strengths and minimise your weaknesses

Callard the PLAYER

As a player, I had previously had a very successful season, playing all of the league matches and then featuring in a cup triumph at Twickenham. This triumph was a record. We won the match by a score of 48-6, which still stands today for a cup final. All the hard work I had been putting in had paid off, or so I thought.

At the start of the following season I lost my place. In fairness it was to a current international who had made the small hop from our rivals. It was exceptionally hard to take, but I learnt very quickly that the only person who feels sorry for you is yourself.

I analysed the position that I wanted back, what was required, and what I needed to do to get that jersey. I shared my objectives and aims in confidence with one of the fitness coaches and a close friend who was in the side.

This player had worked hard for his position and was willing to share advice. I was also to take courage from his sheer willpower and his bloody mindedness. It gave me great confidence, because he wanted me in the side, not from a friendship perspective, but from a view that I could add value to the team that he wanted to become more successful.

I competed hard for my goal in training, setting aside early mornings for speed and weight sessions, and the evenings for goal kicking and positional skills. These sessions were outside the main club sessions.

I had four clear areas that I wanted to improve:

1. Speed
2. Fitness
3. Kicking
4. Game understanding

Each of the four components was evaluated from my performances in the second-team games. For example, in one I kicked four out of five goals successfully, four from four touch finders, three breaks, and two successful counterattacks. It was also important to evaluate this against the feedback of the coach, who was supporting me.

Other performances were poor, but in my strategy of working hard alongside my profile and what I wanted, I was not going to be deterred. This helped me reclaim my position in the team and hold onto it in the coming years when up-and-coming players posed a challenge to me.

5. Maximising your motivation
6. Monitoring changes that occur over time
7. Highlighting any discrepancies between the coach and the player if both complete a performance profile

Why Isn't There a Standard Performance Profile for All Rugby Players?

Performance profiles should be personal for two reasons. First, the characteristics of a prop forward are far different from those of a winger, so these differences are reflected in the performance profile. Second, the performance profile is based on the experiences and opinions of each person who completes the profile, so you have your own performance profile.

Callard the **COACH**

As a coach you want to encourage players to develop a unique profile, because this is what will set them apart from the rest. Yes, players must do the basics well, but the unique skill sets of players are often what create world-class performers.

Take a prop for example. He or she has to scrummage, lift in the lineout, and hit rucks hard. But if the prop can develop a side step, handle, and produce offloads through the tackle, then he or she has a unique skill range that is likely to allow him or her to stand out from the crowd.

Completing Your Own Performance Profile

Creating your personal performance profile involves (1) identifying the qualities required for success in the position that you play, (2) selecting the most important qualities, and (3) plotting your performance profile and ranking your current level.

Phase 1: Identifying the Qualities

The first phase of completing your performance profile is to list the qualities or characteristics that are crucial for success in players who play in your position. These qualities are categorised as physical, technical, tactical, and psychological (see table 2.1 on page 16).

As such, you should write down the qualities that you believe make up top performances under the appropriate headings in table 2.2 on page 16. Try to generate as many qualities as you can. Consider physical, technical, tactical, and psychological qualities. These characteristics represent a range of likely contributory factors to success in your position.

TABLE 2.1　Physical, Technical, Tactical, and Psychological Self-Assessment Example

Physical	Technical	Tactical	Psychological
Speed	Follow-through in kick	Knowing when to kick the ball and when to run with the ball	Being able to handle pressure
Agility	Shoulder position during tackle	Reading game when opponents are attacking	Mental toughness
Power	Catching high balls	Understanding defensive patterns	Being motivated
Explosive strength for jumping			Concentration levels
Flexibility			Managing aggression
Fitness to last full 80 minutes			Having the correct attitude at all times
Being injury free			
Acceleration from a standing start			

Adapted from R. Butler, 1996, *Performance profiling* (Leeds, UK: National Coaching foundation), 10.

TABLE 2.2　Physical, Technical, Tactical, and Psychological Self-Assessment

Physical	Technical	Tactical	Psychological

From A. Nicholls and J. Callard, 2012, *Focused for rugby* (Champaign, IL: Human Kinetics). Adapted from R. Butler, 1996, *Performance profiling* (Leeds, UK: National Coaching Foundation), 10.

Phase 2: Selecting the Most Important Qualities and Defining Their Meaning

Phase 2 of the performance profile involves listing the most important qualities from phase 1 and then writing down what each quality means to you. Table 2.3 is an example of this box being completed by a player who plays in the full back position. You might not agree that this list of 12 qualities is required for a full back, and you may disagree with the definitions of each quality. That is fine.

TABLE 2.3   Meanings Associated With Qualities Example

Quality	Meaning
1. Speed	Being able to run fast
2. Agility	Being able to change direction quickly whilst running
3. Knowing when to kick the ball and when to run with the ball	Having good decision making
4. Being able to handle pressure	Being able to manage stress and make correct decisions even when experiencing stress
5. Mental toughness	Being mentally strong to make decisions and stand by them
6. Power	Being able to break defences by running through people if needed
7. Catching high balls	Taking balls even when opponents are challenging me
8. Concentration levels	Being focused on what I have to do
9. Explosive strength for jumping	Being able to jump high in the air
10. Shoulder position during tackle	Getting my shoulder correctly positioned when tackling
11. Managing aggression	Not letting my anger get the better of me
12. Fitness to last full 80 minutes	Being able to play for the whole game

Adapted from R. Butler, 1996, *Performance profiling* (Leeds, UK: National Coaching Foundation), 15.

You will probably have selected more than 12 qualities in phase 1. Now select the 12 qualities that you think are the most important in determining success. Rank these in order, using 1 to indicate the most important and 12 to signify the least important. After you have written down the quality, write down what that quality means to you in table 2.4. Remember, there are no wrong or right answers.

TABLE 2.4   Meanings Associated With Qualities

Quality	Meaning
1.	
2.	
3.	
4.	
5.	
6.	
7.	
8.	
9.	
10.	
11.	
12.	

From A. Nicholls and J. Callard, 2012, *Focused for rugby* (Champaign, IL: Human Kinetics). Adapted from R. Butler, 1996, *Performance profiling* (Leeds, UK: National Coaching Foundation), 15.

Phase 3: Plotting the Performance Profile

During this phase you list the qualities and then rate yourself on a scale of 1 to 10 by colouring the appropriate boxes. An important point to consider is what a score of 10 means. Assume that 10 is your maximum potential score. After you have completed your profile, write down your action points, which represent what you need to do to achieve targets. An example of a completed performance profile with action points is presented in figure 2.1 on page 20.

After reviewing the completed profile, list the qualities and then rate yourself out of 10 by colouring the appropriate boxes in figure 2.2 on page 21. As with the previous list of action points, consider what a score of 10 means. Again, assume that 10 is your maximum potential score. Alternatively, 10 may be the standard of your opposition.

Callard the COACH

As a club coach, I have asked players to rank themselves against the best in the world at that particular position and explain why those players are the best in the world. Then, I ask them what they do well against their own profile and how they rank themselves against the world-class traits.

Now you have a profile to compete with the purpose of aiming to be the best you can be.

Getting the Most out of Performance Profiling

The performance profile that you have just completed is the starting point, or at least it should be if you want to benefit from completing it. After you have completed the performance profile and the action points, set some goals regarding how much you would like to improve in each quality. For instance, in some of the characteristics you may think that you have reached your potential, but in other areas you might believe that you have a long way to go. Work out what you are going to do. You might be unsure how you could improve certain areas. For instance, you might feel as though you want to improve your explosive strength but are not sure how you would do this. If you are not sure, see an appropriately qualified strength and conditioning expert who will be able to give you a training programme.

Complete the performance profile on a regular basis, say once per month, and monitor any improvements or declines in particular qualities. If, for instance, you spend time working on some of your weaknesses, you may experience a decline in some of the qualities that you were previously stronger at. If this happens, spend time working again on your previously stronger qualities. Continuously monitor your progress throughout the season. If you think that you need to change some of the qualities within your performance profile, do so. Don't be afraid to make changes. Remember that this performance profile is yours alone.

Another way of getting the most out of your performance profile is to ask your coach to rate you on the qualities that you have rated yourself on. In the performance profile in figure 2.3 on page 22, the player's ratings are shaded in gray, whereas coach's opinions of the player are overlayed in a checkered pattern.

Date _____	Ratings									
Quality	**1**	**2**	**3**	**4**	**5**	**6**	**7**	**8**	**9**	**10**
Speed	■	■	■	■	■	■	■	■		
Agility	■	■	■	■	■	■				
Knowing when to kick ball and when to run	■	■								
Being able to handle pressure	■									
Mental toughness	■	■								
Power	■	■	■	■						
Catching high balls	■	■	■	■	■	■	■	■	■	
Concentration levels	■	■	■	■						
Explosive strength for jumping	■	■	■	■	■	■	■	■		
Shoulder position during tackle	■	■	■	■	■	■				
Managing aggression	■	■								
Fitness to last full 80 minutes	■									

Action points

- Need to work on ability to handle pressure by learning some new coping strategies and seeing a sport psychologist. Aim to improve this from 1 to between 6 - 8 within 3 months.

- See conditioning coach about improving fitness from 1 to 5 - 7 months within 2 months.

- Work on being able to direct aggression better. See sport psychologist and aim to improve this from 2 to 8 - 10 within 1 month.

FIGURE 2.1   Performance profile example.

Date _____	Ratings									
Quality	**1**	**2**	**3**	**4**	**5**	**6**	**7**	**8**	**9**	**10**

_____

Action points

-
-
-
-

_____

FIGURE 2.2 **Performance profile.**

From A. Nicholls and J. Callard, 2012, *Focused for rugby* (Champaign, IL: Human Kinetics).

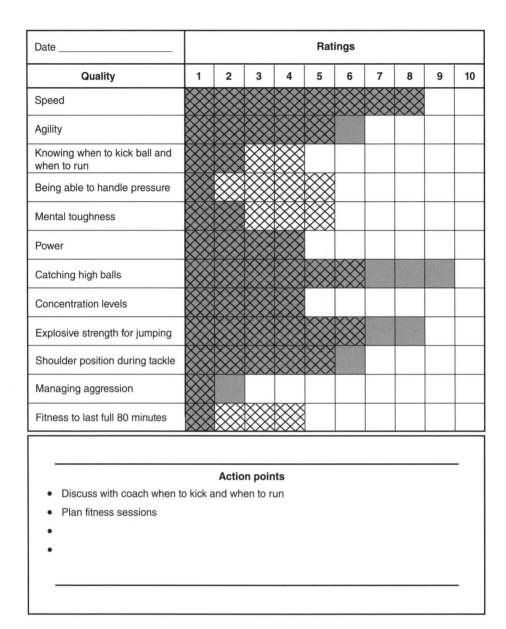

FIGURE 2.3   **Player and coach performance profile example.**

In this example some differences are apparent between the player's ratings and the coach's ratings. For instance, the player rates his agility as a 6, but the coach rates the player's agility as a 5. Another significant difference is in the rating of the player's fitness. The player rates himself at 1, whereas the coach rates the player's fitness at 4. These differences of opinion can lead to a discussion between the player and the coach regarding what the player should work on first. The player may believe that he should work one particular area first, such as his fitness, whereas the coach may believe that the player should first work on managing his aggression.

Creating a More Open Atmosphere for Coach and Athlete Communication

Rugby is a team sport that involves both players and coaches, in addition to sport science and medical staff, who all have a common objective. Research by sport psychologists Dale and Wrisberg (1996) found that the performance profile helped create an atmosphere in which the players and coaches had an opportunity to identify and then discuss areas in need of improvement. In the first task, players are asked to make a performance profile of their views on what makes a successful team. The players could discuss what makes a successful team and the characteristics that contribute to the success of a team. The team can then jointly identify the 12 most important attributes before confidentially rating themselves.

TASK   Players' Views on Successful Teams

Discuss what a successful team is with all members of the squad present. Once a comprehensive definition is established, deliberate the factors that contribute to the success of a team.

In the next task, players share their views on the characteristics of an ideal coach, such as the characteristics of a successful coach, and then narrow these characteristics to the most important ones. The purpose of this exercise is to reduce conflict between the coach and the players.

TASK   Players' Views on an Ideal Coach

Players should brainstorm and identify the 12 most important characteristics of a successful coach. Once these characteristics are indentified, players will rate their coaches in each of the 12 characteristics on a scale of 1 to 10. Players should recognize that this task is an opportunity for them to express the characteristics that define an ideal coach. Also, each player will confidentially rate the coaches in each characteristic. The numbers are totalled and divided by the number of players to produce a mean score for each characteristic.

Finally, in the last task, the players and coaches come together to discuss the profiles and generate an action plan regarding what they can do. Potentially, this could be a confrontational meeting if large discrepancies exist between the views of the coach and the players. Before such a meeting takes place, both the players and coaches must understand that the purpose of the task is to identify areas that can be developed to improve the team atmosphere. Players and coaches must remain calm.

TASK **Athletes and Coach Discuss Performance Profiles**

All players and coaches should be present. Both players and coaches discuss the successful team profile. Coaches can mention different characteristics if they believe it necessary. After that, players and coaches then discuss each rating to discover any discrepancies. An action plan is then generated for how the team can move forward and become a more successful team. Additionally, players and coaches discuss the ideal coach performance profile.

Areas that the coaches scored poorly on are discussed first, and an action plan is generated regarding how the coaches can improve. The team profile and coach profile should be regularly revisited to ensure improvement or work out why the scores on either profile are not improving.

The performance profile of a successful team might look something like the completed performance profile example in figure 2.4 and the performance profile of an ideal coach might look something like the completed performance profile example in figure 2.5 on page 26.

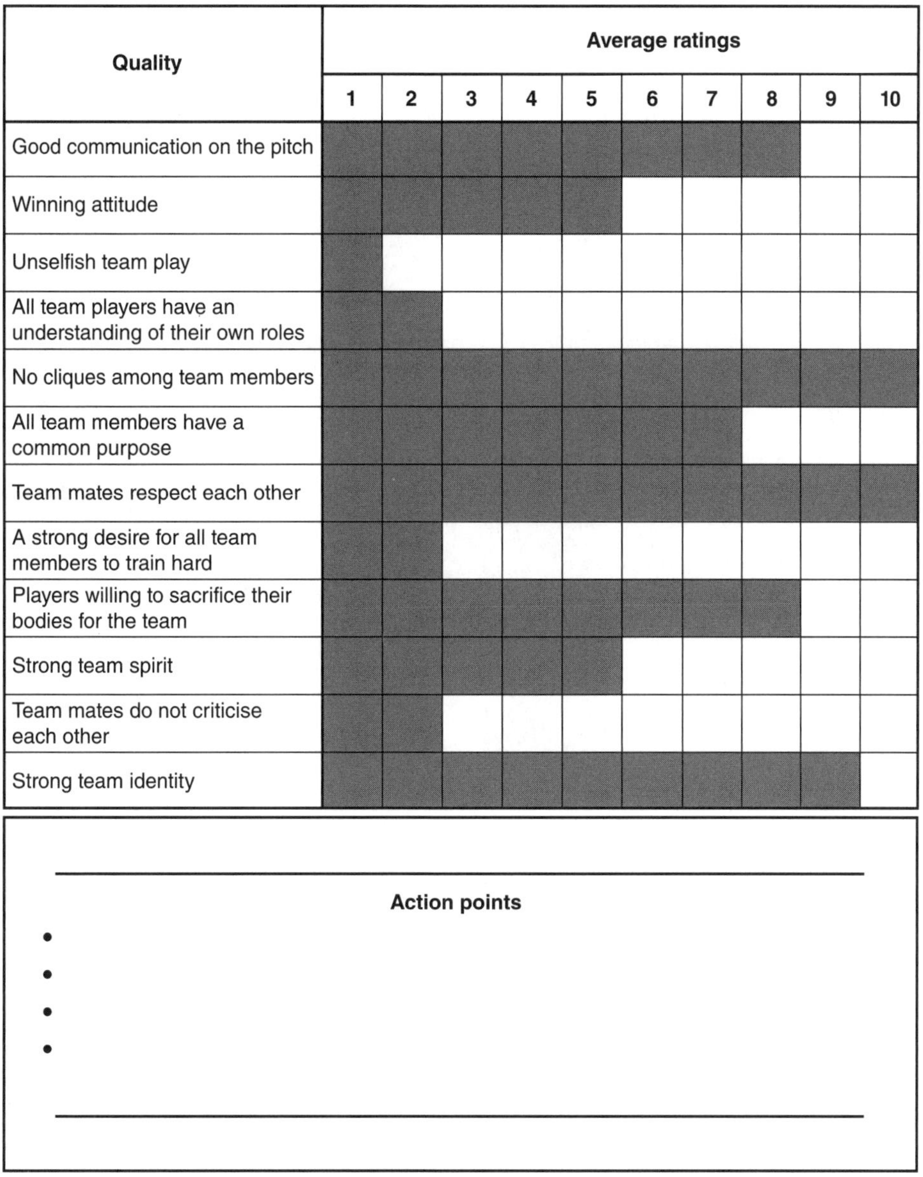

Quality	Average ratings									
	1	2	3	4	5	6	7	8	9	10
Good communication on the pitch	■	■	■	■	■	■	■	■		
Winning attitude	■	■	■	■	■					
Unselfish team play	■									
All team players have an understanding of their own roles	■	■								
No cliques among team members	■	■	■	■	■	■	■	■	■	■
All team members have a common purpose	■	■	■	■	■	■	■			■
Team mates respect each other	■	■	■	■	■	■	■	■	■	■
A strong desire for all team members to train hard	■	■								
Players willing to sacrifice their bodies for the team	■	■	■	■	■	■	■			
Strong team spirit	■	■	■	■	■					
Team mates do not criticise each other	■	■								
Strong team identity	■	■	■	■	■	■	■	■	■	

Action points

-
-
-
-

FIGURE 2.4 **Team performance profile example.**

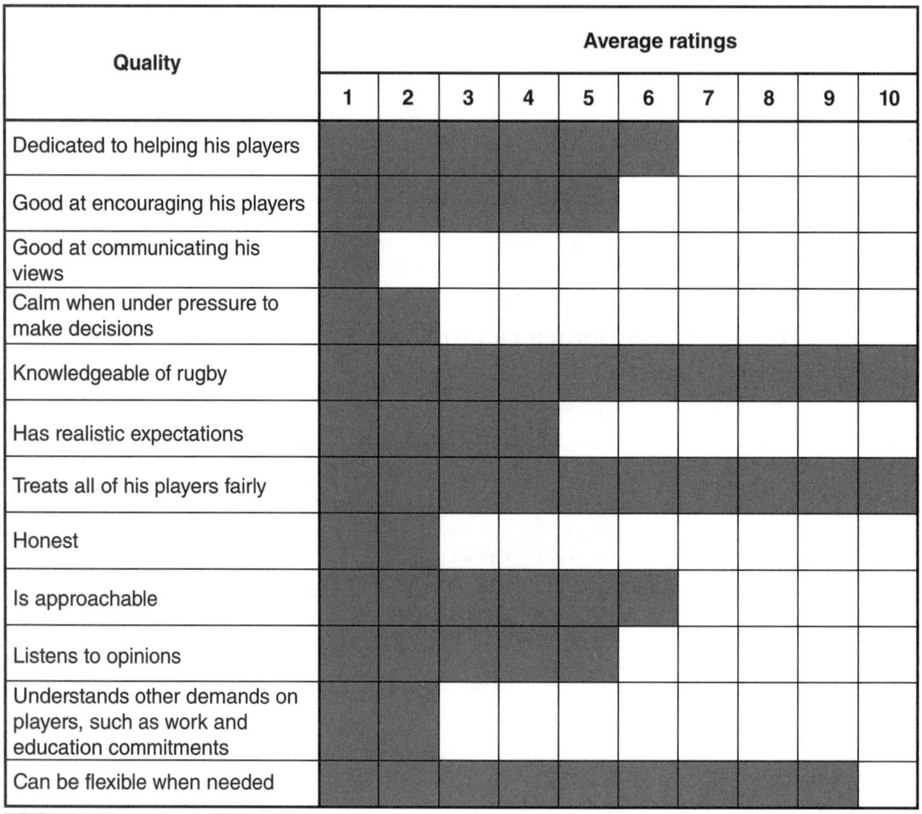

Quality	Average ratings									
	1	2	3	4	5	6	7	8	9	10
Dedicated to helping his players										
Good at encouraging his players										
Good at communicating his views										
Calm when under pressure to make decisions										
Knowledgeable of rugby										
Has realistic expectations										
Treats all of his players fairly										
Honest										
Is approachable										
Listens to opinions										
Understands other demands on players, such as work and education commitments										
Can be flexible when needed										

Action points

-
-
-
-

FIGURE 2.5 Ideal coach performance profile example.

Summary

- The performance profile helps you identify the characteristics required to be successful at rugby.
- If you complete it honestly, the performance profile illustrates your strengths and weaknesses.
- The performance profile highlights which areas of your game you need to work on.
- By completing the performance profile on a regular basis you can monitor improvements that you have made.
- The performance profile can help improve team unity when used in a team setting.
- Remember that many small improvements in many characteristics can result in a large improvement overall. The performance profile is a tool to identify where you need to improve.

CHAPTER 3

Preparing for Peak Performance

I always started the matches slowly. It would often take me 20 minutes or so to get into the game, which was not good enough because I would often make mistakes early on. It is so important to be ready, both mentally and physically, as soon as that whistle goes by preparing properly.

Jonny, British university player

What Is Preparation?

Preparation refers to the processes of ensuring that you are ready for a forthcoming rugby match or training session. As such, this involves the behaviours (e.g., diet, abstinence from alcohol, physical training) and thoughts (e.g., mental practice) that you engage in leading up to a specific event such as a rugby match. Preparation includes the following:

1. **Physical preparation.** Physical preparation refers to the process of ensuring that your body is physically ready for a match, such as (*a*) being warmed up at the start of the match, (*b*) starting the match with optimal energy levels, and (*c*) performing relevant movements in the warm up, such as passing, tacking, and catching.

2. **Mental preparation.** Preparing yourself mentally includes the practices that you engage in to ensure that your mind is ready for the challenge of a rugby match, and can include (*a*) listening to the same music on the way to a match, (*b*) visualising what you want to happen, and (*c*) psyching yourself up or calming yourself down.

Callard the COACH

In the past, games were always on a Saturday around midafternoon. Nowadays, matches are on Friday evenings, Saturdays, and even on Sundays. Players and coaches must be able to adjust and get the preparation needed to optimise performance. Both physical and mental preparation must be correct.

Is Preparation Important, and If So, Why?

The answer is yes. Preparation is extremely important to your performance both in rugby and in other domains of your life. As the old saying goes, 'Fail to prepare, then prepare to fail.'

Preparation is crucial because the best opportunity to score a try in a match might occur in the very first minute or your opponents' best attack might occur within the first minute. You have to be ready from the first whistle either to score that try or to make the try-saving tackle. Optimal physical and mental preparation will ensure that you are ready from the first minute until the last minute.

What Is Poor Preparation?

Poor preparation is not necessarily when an athlete does no preparation whatsoever. A rugby player may attempt to prepare, but the preparation is deemed as being poor when it is inadequate for maximising performance. Poor preparation occurs when you have not gone through the right procedures in time to get yourself ready, either physically or mentally for a particular situation, such as training session or match. Examples of poor physical preparation include not attending training sessions in relation to a forthcoming match, not trying in training, eating a poor diet, or not allowing enough time for your body to recover from alcohol if you drink. Poor mental preparation occurs when you don't spend time thinking about what you want to achieve in a particular match or training session nor spend time thinking about how you are going to achieve your goals. Alternatively, some players have routines that they go through in their minds during build up to matches such as visualising different aspects of the game. An example of poor mental preparation would be a player who usually visualises not bothering with this routine for a particular match.

Why Do Players Sometimes Fail to Prepare?

Some players may ignore physical preparation, others might ignore mental preparation, whereas some players might make any mental or physical preparation in the build up to matches or training sessions. Sometimes players can become complacent with their previous performance and think that because things are going well they don't need to prepare. This is the wrong attitude to adopt. Generally, when rugby players take short cuts in preparation, performance will suffer. Another reason why some players may fail to prepare either mentally or physically is because they are unaware of the importance of both mental and physical preparation.

The Consequences of Poor Preparation

Failing to prepare properly can have a variety of undesirable consequences, which could include:

- Poor performance
- Decreased confidence, as a result of performing poorly
- Increased risk of injury because you might not be mentally alert and ready to impacts
- Increased stress levels as players who don't prepare adequately worry more, because deep down they know they are not ready to perform.

For most of us, there will be instances when we have not prepared as well as we could have done for a match. Think of a match that you did not prepare properly. Write down what you did, if anything, both physically and mentally that contributed to you not preparing properly in table 3.1. Also write the consequences of this poor preparation. For example, you might not have hydrated yourself fully for the match, you might not have warmed up fully, or cut corners in your training in the build to a match. These would be examples of poor physical preparation. Once you have listed your poor physical preparation now list your mental preparation. You might have not have set goals for your upcoming match or focused on what you wanted to accomplish. Then write down what happened in the match, which are the consequences of poor preparation.

TABLE 3.1   A Match in Which You Did Not Prepare Properly

Date of match: _____

Opponents: _____   Competition: _____

Poor physical preparation behaviours	Poor mental preparation	Consequences

From A. Nicholls and J. Callard, 2012, *Focused for rugby* (Champaign, IL: Human Kinetics).

Callard the COACH

It is important to plan well and cover the majority of incidents that could happen in a game to give yourself the best chance of performing well. But you need to get the balance right between underpreparing and overpreparing. Overpreparing can be detrimental to your performance. I have seen international players and club coaches worry about too many things the day before kickoff. They stay on their feet far too long trying to improve themselves and the team. The tank has to be full and the team needs to be full of confidence to play and perform. Less can be best in this situation!

When Do You Start Your Preparation?

Physical preparation for your next game can start immediately after a match when you perform cool-down exercises and stretches, but most of your physical preparation starts during your first training session after your previous game. If you play a match on Saturday and your next training session is on Monday, then this is when you have to step up physically to prepare for your next match. Training represents physical and tactical preparation for matches. But you should also start thinking about your upcoming match before your first training session and ask yourself these questions:

1. What do I want to work on in today's training to be ready for my next match?
2. How I am going to make sure that I practice what I need to practice in training?
3. What do I want to achieve in training this week?
4. What do I want to prevent from happening in training?

Table 3.2 is a sample response to some of these questions regarding your mental preparation for training. After reviewing it, complete table 3.3 with your own answers.

Go into every training session with clear objectives regarding what you want to achieve, so that each training session involves both physical and mental preparation.

TABLE 3.2   Answers to Preparation Questions Example

Question	Answer
What do I want work on in today's training to be ready for my next match?	My passing on Saturday was not as good as it should have been. I need to make sure that I follow through properly when passing. I will ask my coach for advice.
How I am going to make sure that I practice what I need to practice in training?	I will get to practice early and stay behind for additional passing practice if I think that I don't get the practice I need.
What do I want to achieve in training this week?	I want to come away from training feeling positive about my passing and knowing what the team plans are for Saturday's game.
What do I want to prevent from happening in training?	I don't want to go through training not working on anything particular or come away from training not having worked on my passing.

TABLE 3.3   Answers to Preparation Questions

Question	Answer
What do I want work on in today's training to be ready for my next match?	
How I am going to make sure that I practice what I need to practice in training?	
What do I want to achieve in training this week?	
What do I want to prevent from happening in training?	

From A. Nicholls and J. Callard, 2012, *Focused for rugby* (Champaign, IL: Human Kinetics).

Day Before the Match

The day before the match is crucial in determining how well you are going to perform the following day. View the week leading up to the match as the foundation for your performance. A strong foundation is required for maximum performance.

By the time you get to this point you will have been involved in training sessions, barring any injury, and will have completed most of your physical preparation. This is the day to be confident in your physical preparation. Knowing that you have not cut any corners in your physical preparation should give you confidence because you have done everything in your power to ensure that you will be able to perform at your best. If you have cut corners in training, ask yourself why you have done that and work out what you can do to prevent this from occurring in the future. If you continue to cut corners you have to accept that you will never perform to your true potential.

Although most of your physical preparation is complete, especially by the day before the match, your mental preparation becomes more prominent. On the evening of the match spend 10 to 15 minutes mentally imaging these items (see chapter 6 for more information on mental imagery):

- What you want to happen in tomorrow's match
- How you will achieve what you want to happen in tomorrow's match
- How you will play to your strengths
- How you will avoid exposing your weaknesses to your opponents
- Your role within the team
- Various attacking formations
- Defensive patterns

A useful way to start is to write down what you want to happen before you start visualising. Table 3.4 is an example of a completed mental preparation sheet. Complete your own mental preparation questions before visualising (table 3.5).

Do this before each match because the answer to your questions could vary greatly depending previous opponents, the weather, and the way that your coach wants to play.

This 10-minute imagery routine the night before the match should fill you with feelings of confidence and empowerment. Imagery is designed to get you ready for the challenges that lie ahead. It is normal and even a good thing for you to feel slightly apprehensive or nervous on the night before a match, because it shows that you care.

Do not spend more than 10 to 15 minutes visualising at the match because too much imaging can cause feelings of severe anxiety or worry, which can be

TABLE 3.4 Mental Preparation Example

Date of match: _____

Question	Answer
What do you want to happen in tomorrow's match?	I want to throw the ball consistently in the lineout and tackle well in the loose.
How will you make happen what you want to happen in tomorrow's match?	I will prepare well mentally for the game and put myself in positions to make lots of tackles. I am not going to shy away from physical contact.
How you will play to your strengths?	I will get stuck into their forwards.
How you will avoid exposing your weaknesses to your opponents?	I will not get isolated against their backs in open play, because I know that they will be quicker than me. I will make sure to communicate well so that this does not happen.
What is your role within the team?	My role is to throw accurately, be strong in the scrummage, tackle well, and use my leadership qualities.
What is your role in different attacking formations?	As a hooker, I am less involved in some of the set moves, but I have a role to play in drives.
What is your role in different defensive formations?	We have a blitz defence, so I know what I have got to do.

TABLE 3.5 Mental Preparation

Date of match: _____

Question	Answer
What do you want to happen in tomorrow's match?	
How you will make happen what you want to happen in tomorrow's match?	
How you will play to your strengths?	
How you will avoid exposing your weaknesses to your opponents?	
What is your role within the team?	
What is your role in different attacking formations?	
What is your role in different defensive formations?	

From A. Nicholls and J. Callard, 2012, *Focused for rugby* (Champaign, IL: Human Kinetics).

draining and result in mental fatigue. After you complete your visualisation spend the rest of the evening relaxing by doing activities that you enjoy such as reading, watching a film, or viewing your favourite television programme to help you relax and switch off. Do not dwell on the negative things that can happen such as making mistakes or selection issues for future matches, because these thoughts are not constructive. Above all, be confident that you have done everything within your power both physically and mentally for the match the following day. Take confidence from knowing that you have done all the right things.

Callard the COACH

A meeting between the coaches and players was organised the night before the match. This match was probably the biggest game in the club's short history, a cup final at Twickenham against the best cup club side in the country.

We would generally meet the night before a match to reinforce tactics, remind players of their roles and responsibilities, and ease some of the tensions that players get before a game. This was a two-way process for the benefit of both the players and the management.

In this particular meeting, various game scenarios were played out. When I look back at this, I believe that it was the underlying factor in our magnificent performance the next day!

Players, as a group, were asked questions: What happens if we lose the captain in the first five minutes? What happens if we go one score down? What happens if we lose a particular member to the sin bin? What is our focus to get back into the game?

Yes, every coach has these plans and covers all eventualities, but rarely does he or she spend time working in a forum situation with the players to get an understanding from them. This sort of meeting gets total buy-in from the players and allows them to stay on task without being distracted.

We did lose the captain after 3 minutes, and not only that, we lost another influential player after 20! The team remained focused and executed the game plan perfectly. It was the best 40 minutes invested in the working week!

Match Day Mental Preparation: Striking a Balance

Although this book is dedicated to the psychology of rugby, it is well worth mentioning that you need to have enough food in your system by eating the correct diet (see a registered dietician for this information) to give you maximum energy. Make sure as well that you are fully hydrated leading up to the game. Although you may feel too nervous to eat, you must eat and allow time for your body to digest the food that you have eaten.

In preparing yourself mentally, do not spend the whole day leading up to the match thinking about it, because you may waste nervous energy. At the same time, don't wait until the match has started before starting your preparation. You will be far too late!

Start your mental preparation before the match starts. Rugby is often considered a game of two halves, and rightly so because a rugby match consists of a first and second half. But if you view rugby as just a game of two halves, you could be missing out on mental preparation time that you can do before the match (prematch) and mental preparation that you can do during halftime. View the warm-up session before the match as when the match really starts; it is a time when you begin gearing up for what lies ahead. You should also mentally prepare during halftime. As such, you could view your preparation for rugby matches as a game of four quarters: prematch, first-half set plays, halftime, and second-half set plays.

Break your preparation down into these four quarters: prematch (table 3.6 on page 38), first-half set plays (table 3.7 on page 39), halftime (table 3.8 on page 40), and second-half set plays (table 3.9 on page 40). Figure 3.1 on page 41 gives you a visual representation of how this time breaks down.

Sport the Library

Wales's well-documented preparation and determination for the 2011 World Cup allowed them to perform at their very best, as illustrated by Jamie Roberts fighting past an opponent.

TABLE 3.6   Mental Preparation Schedule: Prematch

Period	PREPARATION STRATEGIES	
	Do's	Don'ts
On the coach or in the car travelling to the match	Establish a routine—listen to your favourite album or collection of songs on the way to the ground. Start to associate these songs with playing rugby.	Don't spend all of your journey thinking about the match, because you will waste mental energy. If you find that you can't stop thinking about the match, distract yourself by talking to your teammates, listening to music, or even reading a magazine or book.
	If you are on the coach, enjoy the company of your team-mates.	
	Be confident in your physical and mental preparation leading up to this point.	
	Enjoy the nervous anticipation of playing competitive rugby.	
	During the last 10 minutes of your journey start warming up mentally. Visualise yourself doing various rugby skills such as tackles, passes, kicks, lineout jumps, and so on.	
Arriving at the ground and in the changing room	After you arrive at the ground, let your concentration start to narrow on the roles that you are going to perform during the match (e.g., kicking, scrimmaging, lineout jumping, catching high balls, and so on).	Don't anticipate the result of your match or dwell on previous matches that you have played.
	As you get changed into your rugby clothing, start getting into your game mind-set.	
	Think about what you are going to do in the match and how you are going to make it happen.	
	Communicate with other players in a positive manner.	
During the prematch warm-up	Go through your normal physical prematch routine.	Don't just go through the motions when warming up before the match starts. Have intensity about everything that you do during this phase.
	Do everything in the warm-up the same as you will in the match. If you use routines in a match, use them during this phase, such as kicking routines.	

(continued)

	PREPARATION STRATEGIES	
Period	Do's	Don'ts
In the changing room just before the match starts	Some players play better when they get psyched up, whereas others prefer to be calm just before the match starts. Know what suits you best. If you prefer to be calm, stay away from the players who psyche themselves up. If you play better when you are psyched up, be close to the players in the changing room who do this.	Don't think about mistakes. Everyone makes mistakes. If you make a mistake, refocus your concentration on your role.
	Spend a couple of minutes going through your roles and how you will respond to various scenarios that might happen.	
	Be confident about your mental and physical preparation.	
	Help your teammates by making positive statements.	
	Most important, remember to enjoy your match!	

TABLE 3.7 Mental Preparation Schedule: First-Half Set Plays

	PREPARATION STRATEGIES	
Period	Do's	Don'ts
First half of the match	During breaks in play and before set plays (scrums, lineouts, penalty kicks) focus on your role and want you want to make happen.	Don't dwell on mistakes during breaks in play.

TABLE 3.8   Mental Preparation Schedule: Halftime

Period	PREPARATION STRATEGIES	
	Do's	Don'ts
Halftime break in the changing rooms	Visualise three things that you have done well.	Don't switch off completely. Remember that you are going to be back out playing within 10 minutes or so.
	Focus on what you want to achieve during the next 40 minutes of the second half and how you will achieve that.	Don't focus only on mistakes that you may have made.
	Start the second half knowing exactly what you want to do and how you are going to make it happen.	
	Narrow your focus as the second half ends and switch on again as you leave the changing rooms.	Don't worry about whether you will be substituted or not.
	Be ready from the very start of the second half.	

TABLE 3.9   Mental Preparation Schedule: Second-Half Set Plays

Period	PREPARATION STRATEGIES	
	Do's	Don'ts
Second half of the match	During breaks in play and before set plays (scrums, line-outs, penalty kicks), focus on your role and want you want to make happen.	Don't dwell on mistakes during breaks in play.

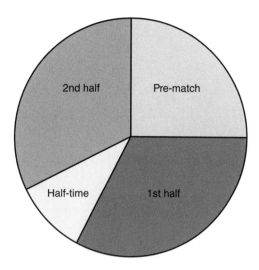

FIGURE 3.1 **The four quarters of preparation.**

Summary

- Preparation refers to the process of getting yourself physically and mentally ready for a rugby match or training session.
- Preparation is crucial for optimal performance.
- Start your preparation early.
- Find out what works for you, and stick to your performance routine.

CHAPTER 4

Developing Mental Toughness

It was a tough situation. We had two games left, and we all knew that we needed two wins to avoid relegation. Deep down I knew we would win those remaining games—there was no doubt in my mind. I also knew that I would have to make a strong contribution in both matches, and I was ready to do it.

Steve, current professional player

What Is Mental Toughness?

Most coaches and athletes believe that mental toughness is one of the most important psychological characteristics that determine success in rugby. Mental toughness is a widely used, but often misunderstood, term. People who are mentally tough have complete self-belief in their own ability, an unshakable faith that they are in complete control of their own destiny, and a conviction that they will be relatively unaffected by setbacks.

Callard the COACH

People often misunderstand the distinction between mental toughness and physical toughness. Physical toughness is about being strong, abrasive, and unrelenting in a physical performance. Players performing with injuries and battling through the pain are often referred to as being mentally tough. I agree in part, but mental toughness is about players who can handle their minds in high-pressure situations—the two-on-one pass in the corner, the last-minute pressure kick to win the game, or the crucial lineout throw to the jumper to secure possession. All are simple examples of the mind being in control of the situation, thus allowing the body to perform its function well and remain undistracted.

Four Cs of Mental Toughness

Mental toughness consists of the 4 Cs: control, commitment, challenge, and confidence (Clough, Earle, & Sewell, 2002).

- **Control.** People who are mentally tough are not afraid to take control or responsibility for the situation that they are in.
- **Commitment.** Mentally tough individuals involve themselves fully in what they are doing and always give maximum effort.
- **Challenge.** The athlete who is mentally tough views all stressful situations as being challenging and focuses on what can be gained from stressful situations (e.g., enhancing reputation, scoring a try, winning the match).
- **Confidence.** The most mentally tough rugby players have an immensely strong belief in their ability to achieve success.

The four Cs are the foundations of mental toughness. Researchers have also identified a number of traits and behaviours that are associated with mental toughness (see figure 4.1).

Callard the PLAYER

I kept in *control* during pressure situations in games by using triggers in my head. It worked and allowed me to control situations that were thrust upon me. I was lucky to play in the same side as some very courageous and committed players. I used to thrive off them, and I did not want to let them down—that was the basis for my *commitment*. When it was tough, in both training and matches, I used to recount to myself, 'If it was easy, everyone would be doing it!' Also, you need to have a clear focus of where you want to be and how you are going to get there. It has to mean something, something of huge value that you would sacrifice all for. It has to *challenge* you. Additionally, it becomes a habit, an addiction, the ability to win games in the severest situations, but it also comes from *confidence*, as teams will play knowing that they will only beat themselves by imploding.

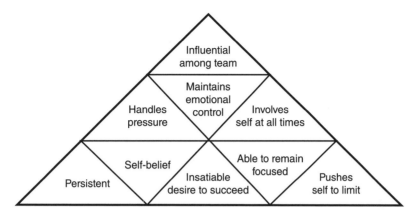

FIGURE 4.1 Traits and behaviors associated with mental toughness.
Sources: Clough, Earle, and Sewell 2002; Jones, Hanton, and Connaughton 2007.

Becoming More Mentally Tough

We have now explained what mental toughness is, and you might now be asking yourself what you can do to become more mentally tough. Researchers have investigated the strategies and behaviours of the most mentally tough athletes. You can improve your mental toughness by

1. adopting the mind-set, attitude, and behaviour of a mentally tough rugby player and
2. engaging in the strategies used by the most mentally tough athletes.

Callard the COACH

Wanting to be mentally tough is not something that happens overnight. You have to work on it, you have to be inspired to want to do it, and more important, you must have a desire to do it. This is something you cannot bluff, something you cannot turn on and off. You have to develop it deep inside.

I have seen some great champion-winning sides that prepare the mind for the mental battle through sheer physical endeavour. I had the pleasure of watching one of the South African Super 14 sides train in preseason. The players were 'flogged.' They ran to the point of physical despair and were then asked to perform the skill of a drill under intense duress straight after. They worked on the mantra 'If the body can sustain the exterior bashing, it can protect the encased computer that will remain always undamaged.' In that following season they won the championship again. In no fewer than eight matches they managed to win the game in the last few minutes! Yes, they were physically strong, but they were mentally strong enough to complete and defend plays to the final whistle, too. The players had the mind-set, attitude, and behaviour of being mentally tough.

TASK Adopting the Mind-Set, Attitude, and Behaviour of a Mentally Tough Rugby Player

Now that you understand what mental toughness is, complete the following task.

Identifying a Mentally Tough Player

1. Think about the most mentally tough player who plays in your position, either your favourite international or a local opponent.

2. List the player's behaviours on the rugby pitch.

3. Describe the body language of this player.

4. Describe the attitude of this player.

Mentally tough players, such as England's Maggie Alphonsi, thrive on competition and its challenges.

Icon Sports Media

An example of the behaviours, body language, and attitude of a mentally tough player is presented in table 4.1.

Complete your own lists in table 4.2. After you have listed the behaviours, body language, and attitude of your favourite player, you can model yourself on this player. Adopt the same behaviours, body language, and attitude. For instance, if your favourite player does not reveal his or her emotions when on the pitch, do the same thing the next time that you train or play.

TABLE 4.1 Behaviours, Body Language, and Attitude of a Mentally Tough Rugby Player Example

Position: Hooker   Name of player: A.N. Other

Behaviours	Body language	Attitude
Never hides in a match	Does not let shoulders drop, even after making a mistake	Gives 100% commitment at all times during training and matches
Communicates well with other players	Displays confidence by the way that he or she walks	Never gives up
Is the first to congratulate other players	Does not show emotions—people never really know what he or she is thinking	Enjoys winning but is not afraid to lose
Always encourages teammates	Always keeps his or her head up	Self-assured

TABLE 4.2 Behaviours, Body Language, and Attitude of a Mentally Tough Rugby Player

Position: _____   Name of player: _____

Behaviours	Body language	Attitude

From A. Nicholls and J. Callard, 2012, *Focused for rugby* (Champaign, IL: Human Kinetics).

Be Optimistic

Recent research has suggested that the most mentally tough athletes are the most optimistic (Nicholls, Polman, Levy, & Backhouse, 2008). Optimism refers to the hopefulness and confidence that you have regarding any uncertain outcomes, such as winning a match or being selected for a team. You can become more optimistic by following the ABCDE of learned optimism.

ABCDE of Learned Optimism

A = Adversity: During times of stress, such as after dropping a high ball or missing a tackle on the left shoulder, we encounter difficulty or adversity.

B = Beliefs: We think about the mistake that we have made, which can shape our beliefs. For example, if you have missed four tackles on your left shoulder, you may believe that you are poor at tackling on this shoulder.

C = Consequences: All beliefs have consequences. The consequence of your believing that you are poor at tackling on your left shoulder could be that you try to avoid situations in which you have to tackle using this shoulder. Alternatively, you could attempt to tackle with your right shoulder even when doing so would not be correct.

D = Disputation: To remain optimistic during adversity, dispute your negative beliefs.

E = Evidence: Find evidence to dispute your negative beliefs. Using the example of the player who missed tackles on the left shoulder, you should remember instances when you made successful tackles using your left shoulder.

Don't Be Pessimistic

The most pessimistic athletes are the least mentally tough. Highly pessimistic people tend to lack confidence and always predict the worst when facing any uncertainty in matches or training. Pessimists view a setback such as being dropped or an opponent's scoring a try in a different way than optimistic rugby players do. Pessimistic rugby players blame themselves and their own ability for the setback. Pessimists often think, *I am not good enough* or *None of the other players want me in the team.*

TASK Applying the ABCDE of Learned Optimism

Think about an occasion in a match when you experienced adversity from making a mistake or from being criticised by your coach, which reduced your optimism. An example of such an incidence is presented in table 4.3.

TABLE 4.3   ABCDE of Learned Optimism in Rugby Example

Question	Your answer
Adversity: What happened?	I missed a tackle in the first minute of a match, and the opposing team scored.
Beliefs: What were your beliefs at that point in the match?	I just believed that it was going to be one of those days where everything would go wrong for me.
Consequences: What were the consequences of those beliefs during the match?	I did not try as hard for the rest of the match because I thought that we were going to lose.
Disputation: How would you now dispute those thoughts if it happened again?	I would say to myself, 'Just because they scored in the first minute, it does not mean that we will lose. We have 79 minutes to score more points than they do.'
Evidence: What evidence do you have?	I would think about times when other teams have scored first and we have won anyway.

Now apply the ABCDE of learned optimism by completing table 4.4.

TABLE 4.4   ABCDE of Learned Optimism in Rugby

Question	Your answer
Adversity: What happened?	
Beliefs: What were your beliefs at that point in the match?	
Consequences: What were the consequences of those beliefs during the match?	
Disputation: How would you now dispute those thoughts if it happened again?	
Evidence: What evidence do you have?	

From A. Nicholls and J. Callard, 2012, *Focused for rugby* (Champaign, IL: Human Kinetics).

Three Ps of Pessimism

P = Personal: Pessimists believe that any misfortune they encounter lies within themselves rather than being external, so the misfortune is personal.

P = Permanent: Pessimists also believe that their misfortune is long lasting, or permanent (e.g., *I will always drop high balls*).

P = Pervasive: Pessimists believe that their misfortune is pervasive in all parts of their life and that if they experience misfortune in one part of their life, they will experience it in others.

To maximise your levels of mental toughness, you must avoid adopting a pessimistic mind-set. To accomplish this, do the following:

- Attribute any setbacks that occur to external sources (e.g., the wind for a missed conversion in rugby or the speed of an opponent for a missed tackle).
- View all setbacks as temporary and tell yourself that they are temporary because you can improve your technique to prevent such setbacks from occurring regularly.
- Segment the various parts of your life (e.g., work or school, family, rugby) and understand that a setback that occurs in one part of your life need not influence another part of it.
- Choose to think positively!

Engaging in the Strategies Used by the Most Mentally Tough Athletes

The most mentally tough athletes use strategies such as effort expenditure, thought control, relaxation, and logical analysis. To improve your mental toughness levels, you can start using the strategies presented in table 4.5.

To enhance your levels of mental toughness, practice the strategies used by mentally tough athletes on a regular basis. Besides using these strategies, you should avoid using strategies such as distancing, mental distraction, and resignation (see table 4.6). Even when you experience immense stress, especially during stressful competitive encounters, do not use these strategies even though you may be tempted to do so because they may be the easier option. To be a mentally tough athlete, you cannot take the easy option!

TABLE 4.5   Strategies Used by the Most Mentally Tough Athletes

Coping strategy	What you can do
Effort expenditure	When playing rugby, commit to your performance and always give 100 percent effort regardless of the score, whether it is the first or last minute of a match or a training session.
Thought control	Don't dwell on negative thoughts (e.g., *We are going to lose this match* or *That was a really bad tackle*). Instead, replace negative thoughts with positive thoughts (e.g., *We can win this match if we stick to our plan* or *I am going to catch the next high ball*).
Relaxation	Relax at appropriate times during training and matches, such as during breaks for set plays. Stretch your muscles to avoid any unwanted tension and do breathing exercises (e.g., inhale for a count of four and exhale to a count of eight).
Logical analysis	Analyse your past performances and weaknesses of opponents. Think about possible solutions to any potential problems before competing and analyse the demands of the competition.

TABLE 4.6   Strategies Used by the Least Mentally Tough Athletes: How Not to Cope!

Coping strategy	Description of coping strategy to avoid
Distancing	Distancing refers to removing yourself from a match or training session. This strategy includes walking away from an opponent or a coach during a match or not engaging in conversation with team-mates during training.
Mental distraction	This strategy refers to thinking about things that are not related to the rugby match or training session that you are engaged in (e.g., exam results, work, or relationship difficulties).
Resignation	Accepting that you are not going to achieve your goals, letting yourself feel hopeless and discouraged, wishing that the competition would end immediately, and ceasing to believe in your ability to achieve your goals are examples of resignation coping.

Summary

- Mental toughness is characterised by the four Cs: control, commitment, challenge, and confidence.
- Develop your mental toughness by adopting the behaviour, mind-set, and attitude of a mentally tough rugby player.
- Be optimistic; view adversity as a challenge.
- Refrain from engaging in pessimistic thoughts.
- Use the strategies that the most mentally tough athletes rely on and refrain from using the strategies employed by the least mentally tough.

CHAPTER 5

Coping Effectively With Stress

I could feel my heart pounding in my chest and the tightness in my shoulders. We had a lineout near our try line, and I needed to hit the lineout jumpers with my throw, so we could get the ball to our fly-half and clear it. I blocked the negative thoughts, visualised a successful throw, took a deep breath, and threw the ball in.

Matthew, semiprofessional hooker

What Is Stress?

The physical and mental responses to events that cause us to experience physiological or mental tension are referred to as stress. Experiencing stress can be unpleasant, and stress can negatively affect your performance if you don't manage it effectively.

Callard the PLAYER

Stress is good; it is the driver that pushes athletes beyond themselves to reach the pinnacles of sporting excellence. I loved it—loved it in training and loved it in matches. Yes, it raised the pulse, gave me a dry mouth, and physically made me shake at times, but it gave me a great indication of where I was as a player. I enjoyed the big games because they didn't come around that often. They were there to be enjoyed, if you had time.

What Are the Symptoms of Stress?

When we experience stress, we encounter many different sensations. In addition, people vary in the symptoms of stress that they experience. Some of these symptoms are listed below.

- Increased heart rate
- Muscle tension
- Dry mouth
- Increased blood pressure
- Nausea
- Worry

Why Do We Experience Stress?

Stress occurs when we perceive that the demands of a particular situation, such as the quality of the opponents in a rugby match, outweigh our personal resources to manage the situation. This circumstance is represented as the seesaw diagram in figure 5.1 (Lazarus, 1999).

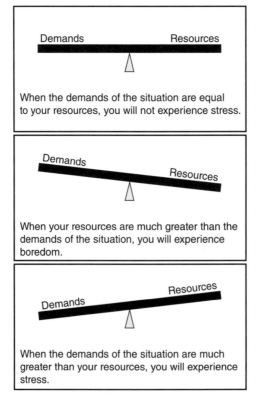

FIGURE 5.1   **Stress seesaw.**

Adapted from R.S. Lazarus, 1999, *Stress and emotion: A new synthesis* (New York: Springer), 59.

In part 1, the demands of the situation and your resources to deal with the stress are similar, so in this instance you would not experience stress. In part 2, your resources to manage the situation are much greater than the demands, so you will experience boredom. In part 3, the demands of the situation are much greater than your resources, so you will experience stress.

Only things that we care about have the potential to cause us stress. For instance, if you don't care about how well you do in a particular exam, that exam will never cause stress. On the other hand, if you do care about your performance in an exam, you may experience stress if you think that you might fail or if you do actually fail. This idea is supported by a quotation from an international rugby player who described his feelings when making his international debut:

> When I played for Wales my first cap was against South Africa, which is one of the best second rows you are going to play against. That was really nerve racking as I sat on the bench thinking, *Oh crap, oh God, there are 80,000 people watching you, live TV cameras*. I was thinking, *I am going against these two awesome guys*. I was bricking it when I went on. I was worried about letting myself down. I did not want to miss a tackle, drop the ball. I did not want to do something stupid knowing that all my friends and family were watching. It was live on TV and my first cap and I was really nervous (Nicholls, Levy, Jones, Rengamani, & Polman, 2011, p. 84).

In this situation, a number of factors caused this player to experience stress, such as playing against well-respected opponents, fear of letting himself down, fear of making a mistake, and the match being televised.

Lynne Cameron/PA Archive/Press Association Images

Players like South Africa's Bismarck du Plessis are often faced with high-pressure situations, and being able to cope with stress helps facilitate successful outcomes.

Stress–Performance Relationship

There is a direct relationship between how effectively people cope with stress and how well they perform (Haney & Long, 1995). That is, when rugby players experience stress but do not cope with it effectively, they experience a decline in performance as their stress levels increase (see figure 5.2a). But when rugby players cope effectively with stress, their performance does not decline (see figure 5.2b). Coping with stress is therefore essential to rugby players.

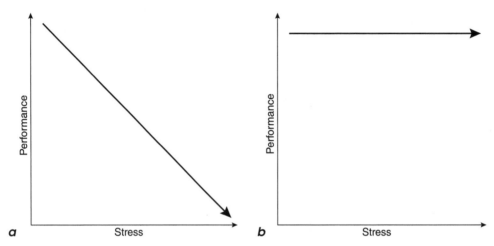

FIGURE 5.2 *(a)* **The performance-stress relationship when ineffective coping strategies are used.** *(b)* **The performance-stress relationship when effective coping strategies are used.**

What is coping? Coping refers to the things that we do to manage stress. It is generally accepted that coping comprises two elements:

- **Cognitive.** Coping that involves mental processes is known as cognitive coping. Strategies include visualisation, blocking out negative thoughts, and wishful thinking.
- **Behavioural.** Coping that involves physical behaviours such as walking away from a stressful encounter is referred to as behavioural coping.

Callard the PLAYER

I dropped an easy high ball and conceded a soft scrum to the opposition. I calmed myself down by taking a deep breath and making sure that my next touch was positive for the team. It was an easy clearance kick from a spilled attack. I picked my spot and buried it into the stand beyond the halfway line.

Coping Effectiveness

Coping effectiveness relates to the degree of success that a coping strategy has in reducing the level of stress that you experience. If deploying a strategy reduces your level of stress, then you are coping effectively, whereas if the intensity of the stress that you experience does not diminish or it increases, your coping strategy is not effective.

Callard the PLAYER

When I had a poor moment, I would stay in control and focus on the next play. There were many moments when I thought I was going to implode inside, but by being focused and making sure that my next involvement was positive, I would get back on track within the game.

Coping More Effectively by Taking Control of Stress

To cope more effectively with stress, people should match their coping strategy with the type of stress that they experience (Folkman, 1991). The key to this method of improving your ability to cope is identifying whether you can control the source of stress (e.g., opponents playing well, making a mistake, or the weather). You can directly influence and control some sources of stress, such as your own performance, but you will be unable to control other sources of stress, such as the referee's decisions. Before deciding what coping strategy to deploy, the first question to ask yourself is, 'Can I control the source of stress?' The answer will be yes or no. Then, depending on your answer, you can move on to deploying the appropriate strategy (see figure 5.3).

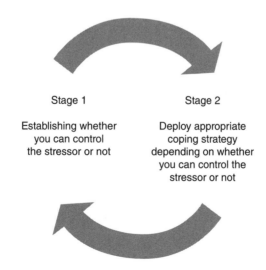

Stage 1

Establishing whether
you can control
the stressor or not

Stage 2

Deploy appropriate
coping strategy
depending on whether
you can control the
stressor or not

FIGURE 5.3 **The two-stage cycle of coping more effectively with stress.**

Two Types of Coping Strategies

If you can control the stressor you should use a problem-focused coping strategy (see figure 5.4). This type of strategy aims at reducing stress by solving a problem. For instance, if your lack of fitness is causing you to worry, you can plan a fitness regime, which is an example of problem-focused coping. By not taking shortcuts in your preparation, you can reduce the likelihood or at least the severity of such stressors by being fully prepared (see chapter 3 for more information on preparation).

Alternatively, if the answer is no and you cannot control the stressor, you should use an emotion-focused coping strategy (see figure 5.5). Emotion-focused coping strategies are directed at reducing your emotional responses to stress. For instance, if the weather is making you anxious you could do some deep breathing to calm yourself down, which is an example of emotion-focused coping. Matching stressors to coping strategies is discussed in detail in the remainder of this chapter.

Stressor and Coping Concept Maps

To understand the concept of stressor controllability and the ways in which you have coped in the past, you should complete your own stressor and coping concept maps and then identify controllable and uncontrollable stressors. An example of a completed map of stressors in rugby is presented in figure 5.6, and the coping strategies used to manage those stressors is presented in figure 5.7 on page 60.

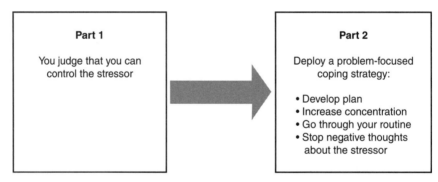

FIGURE 5.4   Coping effectively with controllable stressors.

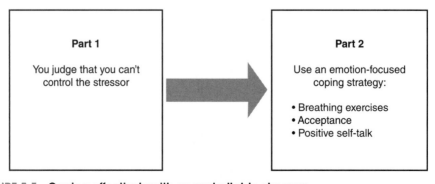

FIGURE 5.5   Coping effectively with uncontrollable stressors.

TASK Complete Your Own Stressor and Coping Maps

The stressors listed in the concept map are best managed by the coping strategies listed in the matching numbered boxes of the coping strategies concept map.

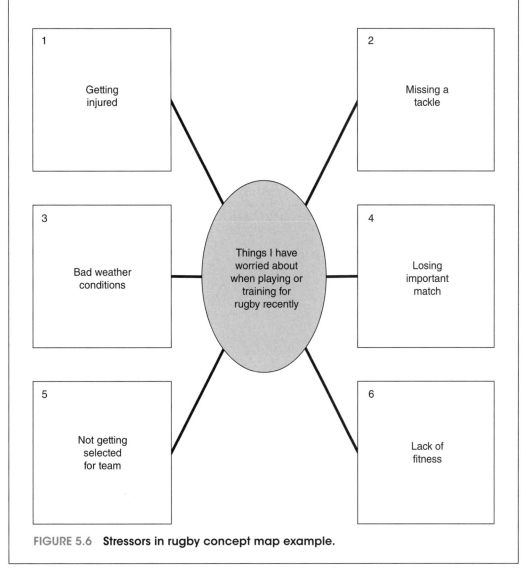

FIGURE 5.6 **Stressors in rugby concept map example.**

(continued)

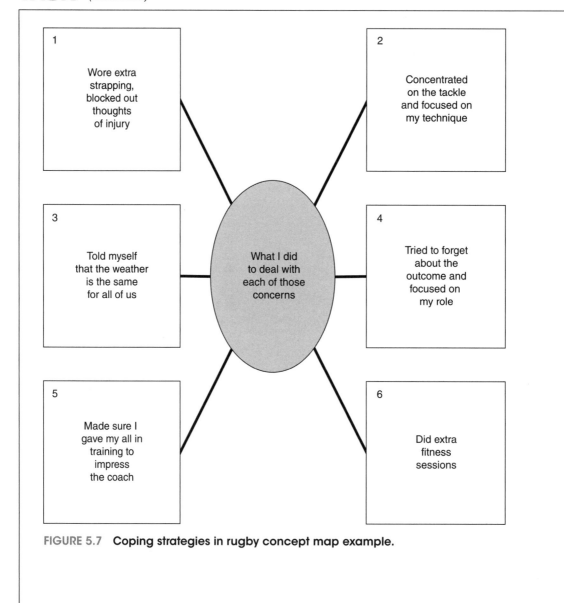

FIGURE 5.7 **Coping strategies in rugby concept map example.**

Stressors in Rugby Concept Map

Now it's your turn. Think about some of the things that you worried about when playing or training for rugby. There are no right or wrong answers. Your opinion is what is important. Describe up to a maximum of six worries in the boxes provided in figure 5.8.

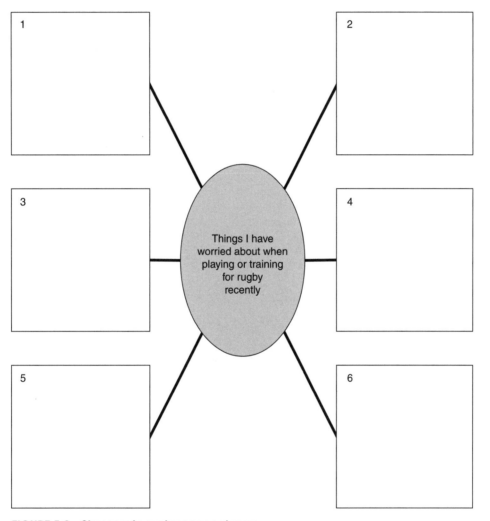

FIGURE 5.8 Stressors in rugby concept map.

From A. Nicholls and J. Callard, 2012, *Focused for rugby* (Champaign, IL: Human Kinetics).

(continued)

Coping Strategies in Rugby Concept Map

Now try to remember what you did to deal with each of the worries that you have just written down. In box 1 of figure 5.9 write how you managed the stressor that you wrote in box 1 of the stressor concept map. In box 2 write what you did to cope with the stressor that you wrote in box 2 of the stressor concept map. Do this for all the boxes.

The coping strategy that you write in box 1 should be the coping strategy that you used to manage the stressor that you listed in box 1 of the stressor concept map. The coping strategy that you write in box 2 of the coping concept map should be the coping strategy that you used to manage the stressor that you wrote in box 2 of the stressor concept map. This applies for all six boxes of the stress and coping concept maps. For example, in figure 5.6 the stressor in box 1 was "Getting injured." The coping strategy used was "Wore extra strapping, blocked out thoughts of injury." In the stressor map the stressor in box 6 was "Lack of fitness." The coping strategy used, written in box 6 of figure 5.7, was "Did extra fitness sessions."

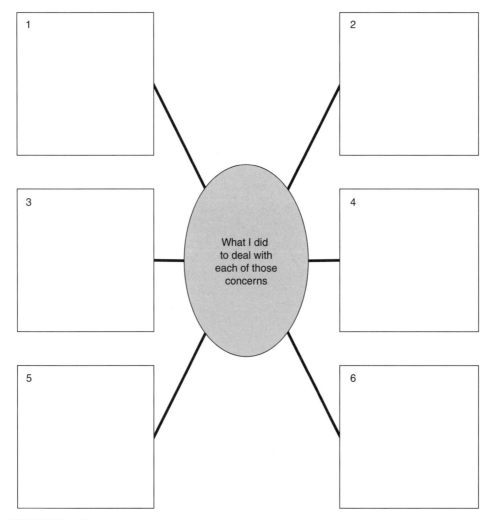

FIGURE 5.9 **Coping strategies in rugby concept map.**

From A. Nicholls and J. Callard, 2012, *Focused for rugby* (Champaign, IL: Human Kinetics).

Identify and Coping With Stressors That You Have Experienced and Can Control

Look at the stressors that you wrote in the stressors in rugby concept map (figure 5.8). Identify the stressors that were directly under your control. A stressor is something that causes you worry, negative emotions, or physiological reactions (e.g., increased heart rate, sweaty palms, muscular tension, nausea, and so on). Table 5.1 lists some sample stressors that are controllable and some that are out of your control.

TABLE 5.1 Controllable and Uncontrollable Stressors

Controllable stressors	Uncontrollable stressors
1. Missing tackles 2. Performing poorly 3. Making poor decisions during matches 4. Fitness worries	1. Team selection 2. Coach criticism 3. Crowd reaction 4. Opponents cheating 5. Teammates 6. Getting injured 7. Weather 8. Opponents playing well 9. Referees making poor decisions

From A. Nicholls and J. Callard, 2012, *Focused for rugby* (Champaign, IL: Human Kinetics).

Remember, controllable stressors are completely within your control and are something that you can influence. List these in table 5.2. If you don't have five controllable stressors from your concept map, think of other controllable stressors that you have experienced.

TABLE 5.2 Identifying Controllable Stressors

	Controllable stressors
1.	
2.	
3.	
4.	
5.	

From A. Nicholls and J. Callard, 2012, *Focused for rugby* (Champaign, IL: Human Kinetics).

To cope more effectively with sources of stress that you can control, you should use problem-focused coping strategies. Problem-focused coping strategies involve strategies that are directed at solving the problem. When the problem has been alleviated, the stress that you experience disappears. Table 5.3 lists some problem-focused coping strategies that you can use when you can control the source of stress.

TABLE 5.3   Problem-Focused Coping Strategies

Coping strategy	How to use this coping strategy
Developing a plan of action to eliminate stressors	The initial coping strategy that you should use to manage controllable stressors such as performing poorly, making mistakes, or even being at an inadequate fitness level should be to create a plan of action. For example, if you have been performing poorly (controllable stressor) because you are using poor technique in a particular skill such as tackling, you can plan additional sessions to improve your tackling technique. This approach could involve consulting with your coach about how you can improve your tackling.
Concentration	During stressful times it can often be difficult to concentrate. One useful method to improve concentration is to use cue words, which you say quietly to yourself. The two types of cue words are instructional and motivational.
	▪ Instructional cue words are technical and relate to a specific aspect of your technique. For example, a rugby player may use the word "body" relating to body position and "drive" referring to the drive phase when tackling. Motivational cue words refer to the psychological state that you want to experience and may include words such as "relaxed," "aggression," or "focused."
	▪ Write a list of words and pick two that you think are important to the area of the game that you want to improve (e.g., lineout throwing, kicking, passing, tackling). The next time that you train or play competitively, say these cue words to yourself as you are about to perform the skill and see how your concentration improves. Practise saying your cue words to yourself.
Routines	For many years athletes from all sports, including rugby, have spoken about the importance of developing and adhering to routines. These routines give you something to fall back on when you experience stress. You should develop your own routine going into matches and for events that occur during matches so that you can prepare mentally and physically.
Stop negative thoughts	Most sport psychologists believe that negative thoughts can be damaging to sporting performance. You should therefore nip negative thoughts in the bud, before they damage your rugby performance. When the negative thoughts occur, close your eyes and visualise a stop sign. Then say the word "Stop" either aloud or to yourself. After you have stopped the negative thoughts, use your two cue words to help your concentration.

Identifying and Coping With Stressors That You Have Experienced and Cannot Control

Similarly, look at the stressors that you wrote in the stressors concept map and identify those that you could not control. Remember, uncontrollable sources of stress are not within your control, so you can do nothing to influence them. List those in table 5.4. Think of other uncontrollable stressors if you do not have five uncontrollable stressors from the concept map that you completed.

TABLE 5.4	Identifying Uncontrollable Stressors

	Uncontrollable stressors
1.	
2.	
3.	
4.	
5.	

From A. Nicholls and J. Callard, 2012, *Focused for rugby* (Champaign, IL: Human Kinetics).

Experiencing a source of stress that you cannot control can be one of the most distressing experiences in sport and life in general. You may feel a sense of powerlessness because there is nothing you can do to manage the stress. In stressful situations such as these, you should use emotion-focused coping strategies. These strategies are directed specifically at managing the emotional distress that you experience whilst playing sport. As such, you are taking control of your emotional reactions to the source of stress, rather than trying to eliminate the stress. Table 5.5 on page 66 shows you a range of emotion-focused coping strategies.

Seeking Support to Manage Controllable and Uncontrollable Sources of Stress

As a rugby player, the people around you are crucial to your success and emotional well-being. These people may include parents, partners, coaches, friends, work colleagues, or children. Anybody who is close to you will have often provided you with support during sport. Certain people that you know, however, will be better at giving you emotional support, whereas others might be better at providing you with problem-solving solutions (see figure 5.10 on page 67). Quite often, the people who are better at providing support to solving problems will not be as helpful in providing emotional support.

TABLE 5.5   Emotion-Focused Coping Strategies

Coping strategy	How to use this coping strategy
Breathing techniques	Athletes have used a variety of breathing techniques for many years. These techniques can be extremely effective in eliminating negative emotional reactions to stress. You should be aware that when people experience stress, most tend to hold their breath or not breathe as often, which makes the symptoms worse! Therefore, you must breathe correctly during times of stress. To do this, follow this exercise: ▪ Pretend that you your lungs are divided into three equal levels: bottom, middle, and top. ▪ Focus your attention on filling the bottom level of your lungs. Do this by pushing your diaphragm down and forcing the abdomen out. ▪ Now fill the middle level of your lungs by expanding your chest and raising your ribs. ▪ Fill the upper level of your lungs by raising your chest and shoulders slightly. ▪ Hold this breath for a few seconds and then exhale slowly by pulling the abdomen in and lowering your shoulders and chest. ▪ Repeat this cycle during periods of stress.
Accept mistakes	A mistake may have negative connotations (e.g., the other team scoring a try), but given that a match lasts 80 minutes you often have time to make up for a mistake. Your reaction to the mistake is what could impede your performance. For example, a kicker might be so frustrated at missing the first kick that he or she misses the second kick as well because of failure to regain his or her composure. You must learn to accept mistakes. This task can be difficult, but after all a mistake is something that has already occurred, so you should not let it influence the rest of your match or training session. After you can fully accept any mistakes you will experience a reduction of negative emotions.
Positive self-talk	When you experience stress that you cannot control, you may tend to dwell on negative thoughts and say things to yourself such as, "They are too good today; there is nothing we can do" or "How am I going to make any goal kicks when it is so windy?" You can change negative self-talk into positive self-talk to empower yourself and experience positive emotions. For example, the statement "They are too good today; there is nothing we can do" could be changed to "They are playing well, but they will not be able to maintain this level of performance for the whole match. As soon as their performance dips, we will be ready to play some of our attacking moves." The other statement, "How am I going to make any goal kicks when it is so windy?" could be changed to "The other fly-half has to kick in the same conditions as I do. I will trust my training, preparation, and technique."

Identifying the People Whom You Turn to for Support During Stressful Times

Write the names of the people whom you turn to for support during stressful times in your life in table 5.6. Don't worry if you don't have five people whom you turn to for support. After you have listed the names of these people, put an "e" beside the person's name if he or she is good at providing emotional support and put a "p" beside the person's name if he or she is good at solving problems. To maximise the support that you receive, speak to the people with an "e" beside their name for problems relating to emotional difficulties and speak to the people with a "p" beside their name when you need advice on solving problems.

Ineffective Coping Strategies

All rugby players will use or have used ineffective coping strategies. Research indicates, however, that athletes are often not aware that what they are doing is ineffective. The most ineffective coping strategies are presented in table 5.7 on page 68.

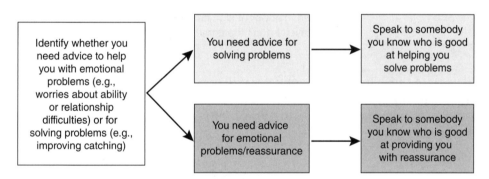

FIGURE 5.10   **Maximising social support.**

TABLE 5.6	Identifying Who You Can Rely on for Support

	Person
1.	
2.	
3.	
4.	
5.	

From A. Nicholls and J. Callard, 2012, *Focused for rugby* (Champaign, IL: Human Kinetics).

TABLE 5.7   Ineffective Coping Strategies

INEFFECTIVE COPING STRATEGIES	
Forcing	Some players attempt plays that they have not practiced before or that do not have a realistic chance of being successful. Whatever level of rugby you play, you must play within your capabilities, especially during times of stress. Do not be tempted to try moves that are completely unrealistic.
Speeding up	Some players speed up their game during periods of stress. If you are involved in lineout throwing or goal kicking in particular, keep your play constant.
Not attempting to cope	Research has revealed that a number of full international rugby players do not attempt to cope in stressful situations. Always attempt to cope. Use a problem-focused coping strategy if you can control the stressor and an emotion-focused strategy if you can't control the stressor.
Focusing on the outcome	Some rugby players focus exclusively on the score of the match or their own statistics (e.g., number of lineout throws missed, goal kicks missed, number of high balls dropped, and so on). Focus on what you have to do in the game, not the outcome.

Be aware of these ineffective coping strategies, but do not fall into the trap of using them during stressful times, no matter how tempting it may be to make no attempt to cope, to force your play, to speed up, or to focus on your performance standard or score.

Summary

- Stress refers to the physical, mental, or emotional responses to events that cause physiological or mental tension.
- There is a direct relationship between how effectively you cope with stress and how well you perform.
- Coping is more effective if you match the coping strategy that you use to the stressor that you encounter.
- When you can control the stressor, use problem-focused coping strategies such as developing a plan, increasing your concentration, going through your routine, or stopping any negative thoughts.
- When you can't control the stressor, use emotion-focused coping strategies such as breathing techniques, acceptance, and positive self-talk.

CHAPTER 6

Using Mental Imagery

*I created a picture in my mind. I knew the exact trajectory
that I wanted the ball to take the moment it left my foot. It was
a very vivid picture in my mind. I knew I could kick the ball
through the posts because the image in my mind was so clear.*

Michael, ex-professional fly-half

What Is Mental Imagery?

Mental imagery refers to the process of using your imagination to see yourself
and feel yourself performing a particular movement (e.g., making a tackle) or
particular skill (e.g., making a pass).

Does mental imagery involve only seeing images? The answer is no. In addition
to seeing images in your mind, your mental imagery should incorporate

- feelings,
- noises, and
- smells.

By incorporating these sensations, your mental imagery will be more realistic
and therefore more beneficial.

Relationship Between Mental Imagery and Sport Performance

Over 200 studies published in the sport psychology literature have provided evidence that mental imagery improves sporting performance. In particular, research
suggests that mentally imagining a particular skill, such as making a lineout throw,
catching a high ball, or goal kicking, can improve your performance of that skill.

Callard the PLAYER

I was big on mental imagery, especially for the position I played. It was huge for me! As a goal kicker I would spend hours rehearsing my routine and kick in my mind, carefully checking the tangible signs that go into a successful action. The plant step is solid, the body looks tall, and my arm is out to the side to balance the action through the point of impact. It included not only what it might look like to the outside world watching but also how it felt to me. I rehearsed both images and feelings.

I can remember in a semifinal of the European Cup at home to Pau. The first half was poor. I had missed a couple of gettable shots at goal. The negative thoughts were starting to creep into my mind. At halftime I took a couple minutes just to rehearse the sequence again and go through my routine. I had done imagery a million times before, but never during halftime. It gave me so much confidence and allowed me to look forward to the next kick with anticipation.

Four theories have attempted to explain how mental imagery improves performance, which we have called (1) muscle memory hypothesis, (2) sequence of movements theory, (3) long-term memory theory, and (4) attentional arousal set theory. These are briefly outlined here:

1. Muscle memory hypothesis. This approach suggests that imaging something creates small innervations in the muscles that you will use for the movement that you are imaging, such as the shoulders and the arms in a lineout throw. If you imagine yourself taking a lineout throw, the muscles used in the movement will become activated. Support for this theory is mixed. Some researchers found increased activity through electromyographic (EMG) machines (Harris & Robinson, 1986), but others found no EMG activity (Mulder et al., 2004). With this in mind, Murphy et al. (2008) suggested that imaging improves performance by priming the nervous system for the muscles that will be recruited when certain actions are performed, such as kicking or passing.

2. Sequence of movements theory. This theory states that imagery helps your performance of skills by allowing you to become more familiar with the sequence of movements involved in performing them. All skills in rugby contain a variety of specific movement patterns that, when combined, form the complete skill. For example, with the goal kick you would (1) plant the nondominant foot, (2) take a back lift of the kicking leg, (3) make a hip rotation, (4) drive the kicking leg through to the ball, and (5) follow-through in a kick. As such, imagery enhances performance by repeatedly activating mental representations of the range of movements that contribute to the overall skill, thus strengthening your memory (Kosslyn et al., 2001).

3. Long-term memory theory. This theory states that all movements are stored as different patterns within your long-term memory, and that imaging different movements strengthens these patterns in your brain. According to Weinberg and Gould (2011), this theory states that images contain *stimulus images* and *response images*. Stimulus images refers to images related to specific scenarios (e.g., people sitting on the sidelines/in the stand, the ball that is going to passed or kicked, or the coach giving a team-talk). Response images are your responses to particular scenarios, such as the physiological responses (e.g., increased heart-rate, feeling of excitement/nervousness, or butterflies in your stomach) when you imagine people standing on the sidelines, having to take a kick, or listening to your pre-match team talk.

4. Attentional arousal set theory. This explanation of how imagery works is not a theory per se; rather, it describes how imagery might help your sport performance by achieving the optimal arousal state. For example, some rugby players play better when they are psyched up and use imagery to psyche themselves up, whereas others might play better when calm and use imagery to calm themselves. Engaging in imagery will help you achieve your optimal mind-set for rugby. Research has indicated that imagery is successful in helping athletes reach the desired arousal level (Hale & Whitehouse, 1998).

At least some evidence supports each of the theories of how imagery can improve performance. In essence, it appears that engaging in imagery triggers nerves in the muscles that you use for various skills and strengthens the movement patterns required for various skills, besides helping you achieve your optimal arousal. Regardless of how imagery does it, the important point to remember is that mental imagery will improve your performance!

Research has indicated that mental imagery has a number of other benefits such as

- enhancing motivation,
- enhancing self-confidence,
- coping with injury and pain, and
- managing stress.

Callard the COACH

I have always talked about the picture I want when I coach and have asked players what various skills look like. I also ask what is needed to paint this picture and what the best way to colour it is. Take the offloading game, for example. This high-paced game has players attacking the holes of the opposition's defence and getting their arms and shoulders through to create passes out of or beyond the tackle. The theory behind an offloading game is that the defence is taken out of its comfort zone and the attacking team get behind it.

The mental picture is pace and fitness with lots of dynamic movement at the line. The paint is the players' ability to off load and produce a variety of passes beyond the line, and the colour is the support lines that go to make an off load successful. They all come together to make the offloading game work. Players practice in small groups first and then are put into a competitive environment with full-on contact. They see the image of a perfectly timed off load executed on the game line with support runners gambling to take the ball forward. They can store this image in their mind and use it within their imagination. A feel and tempo come with it too; it's not just about the sight and the outcome to a player.

I love the expression "See it, read it, and feel it." See where it is to be executed, read the cues to execute it, and the feel your way through the execution. As a coach, the more mental imagery work that you can do with the whole team, the better off you'll be. Imagery gives the team greater understanding of what you want to achieve and how they may want to perform it.

Imagery Perspective: Through Your Own Eyes or on a Television Screen?

When mentally imaging yourself doing a particular skill such as making a last-ditch tackle on an opponent, you can use two different views. These are known as internal and external images.

- **Internal images.** In these images you see what is happening as you would from your own eyes. Essentially, you see exactly what you would be seeing when making a last-ditch tackle (e.g., your opponent running whilst carrying the ball), passing the ball (e.g., the position of your teammates), or catching a high ball (e.g., the ball in the sky).

- **External images.** In external images you see yourself as if you were on television. In an external image of yourself tackling, you would see your whole body making a tackle on your opponent.

People generally prefer one perspective or the other, but it does not matter whether the pictures in your mind are internal images or external images. Both types of images are beneficial to performance. Some athletes use a mixture of internal and external images. If you do this, that is fine as well.

TASK What Type of Imagery Perspective Do You Have?

Think about the last try you scored, tackle you made, or other memorable incident in a match. Re-create this event in your mind using your imagination by doing the following in one minute or so:

- Sit in a comfortable position in a quiet room.
- Close your eyes.
- Re-create the situation in your mind by visualising what you saw, how your body felt, what noises you heard, and what the weather was on the day of the incident.

Question: Did you see the images as they happened to you (internal image), or did you see yourself as though you were looking through a camera lens (external perspective)? Alternatively, you might have struggled to form any images, which means that you need to improve your imagery ability. Imagery ability can be measured, and it can be improved through training. Improving your imagery ability will make mental imagery more effective in enhancing your rugby performance.

Imagery Ability

Nearly everybody can generate images in the mind and engage in mental imagery. But not everybody has the same ability, and some players are better at creating images in their mind. Imagery ability is important, because the better your ability to create images in your mind, the more effective imagery will be in improving your performance. People who can create detailed and controllable pictures in their mind can have the highest imagery ability. You can now measure your imagery ability.

Measuring Your Imagery Ability

To measure your imagery ability, you perform a series of movements and then rate the ease at which you can see images of yourself performing the same movements (questions 1 through 4) and then feel yourself performing the same movements (questions 5 through 8) in the following text.* This method of measuring mental imagery ability has been widely used in the sport psychology literature for the last 40 years. The following series of questions is adapted from a published mental imagery questionnaire called the Movement Imagery Questionnaire–Revised (Hall & Martin, 1997). You may feel self-conscious performing the movements, but this method is the most accurate way of measuring imagery ability and monitoring any changes in imagery ability over time. As you complete the questions, make sure that you answer them honestly!

---

*Adapted from C.R. Hall and K.A. Martin, 1997, "Measuring movement imagery abilities: A revision of the Movement Imagery Questionnaire." *Journal of Mental Imagery* 21(1-2):143-154.

Question 1

Close your eyes and try to *see* yourself moving your arms upward without actually doing it. Rate the ease in which you could see this movement on a scale of 1 to 5, with 5 being very easy to see and 1 being very hard to see.

POSITION 1 Stand with your legs and feet hip-width apart and your arms by your side.

POSITION 2 Raise your arms slowly into the air so that your fingertips are pointing upward.

POSITION 3 Now slowly lower your arms so that they are back by your side in the original starting position.

QUESTION 1

1	2	3	4	5
Very hard to see	Hard to see	Neither easy nor hard to see	Easy to see	Very easy to see

Enter your answer here: _____.

Question 2

Standing back in the original position, close your eyes and try to *feel* yourself raising your right leg. Rate the ease in which you could feel your right leg rising to 90 degrees on a scale of 1 to 5, with 5 being very easy to feel and 1 being very hard to feel.

POSITION 1 **Stand with your legs and feet hip-width apart and your arms by your side.**

POSITION 2 **Raise your right leg slowly into the air until it is 90 degrees to the ground.**

POSITION 3 **Now lower your right leg so that your right foot is back on the ground in its original starting position.**

QUESTION 2				
1	**2**	**3**	**4**	**5**
Very hard to feel	Hard to feel	Neither easy nor hard to feel	Easy to feel	Very easy to feel

Enter your answer here: _____.

Question 3

Close your eyes and try to *see* yourself performing the star jump without actually doing it. Rate the ease in which you could see yourself performing this star jump on a scale of 1 to 5, with 5 being very easy to see and 1 being very hard to see.

POSITION 1 **Stand with your legs and feet hip-width apart and your arms by your side.**

POSITION 2 **Bend down slightly and then do a star jump.**

POSITION 3 **Stand back in the original position.**

QUESTION 3				
1	2	3	4	5
Very hard to see	Hard to see	Neither easy nor hard to see	Easy to see	Very easy to see

Enter your answer here: _____.

Question 4

Close your eyes and try to *feel* yourself moving your left leg and arm out to the side without actually doing it. Rate the ease in which you could feel your left leg and left arm move out to the side on a scale of 1 to 5, with 5 being very easy to feel and 1 being very hard to feel.

POSITION 1 **Stand with your legs and feet hip-width apart and your arms by your side.**

POSITION 2 **Move your left leg and left arm slowly out to the side.**

POSITION 3 **Now lower your left leg and put your left arm back to the starting position so that your left foot is back on the ground and in the original starting position.**

QUESTION 4				
1	2	3	4	5
Very hard to feel	Hard to feel	Neither easy nor hard to feel	Easy to feel	Very easy to feel

Enter your answer here: _____.

Question 5

Standing back in the original position, close your eyes and try to *feel* yourself moving your arms upward without actually doing it. Rate the ease in which you could feel this movement on a scale of 1 to 5, with 5 being very easy to feel and 1 being very hard to feel.

POSITION 1 **Stand with your legs and feet hip-width apart and your arms by your side.**

POSITION 2 **Raise your arms slowly into the air so that your fingertips are pointing upward.**

POSITION 3 **Now slowly lower your arms so that they are back by your side in the original starting position.**

QUESTION 5

1	2	3	4	5
Very hard to feel	Hard to feel	Neither easy nor hard to feel	Easy to feel	Very easy to feel

Enter your answer here: _____.

Question 6

Close your eyes and try to *see* yourself raising your right leg to 90 degrees without actually doing it. Rate the ease in which you could see your right leg rising to 90 degrees on a scale of 1 to 5, with 5 being very easy to see and 1 being very hard to see.

POSITION 1 Stand with your legs and feet hip-width apart and your arms by your side.

POSITION 2 Raise your right leg slowly into the air until it is 90 degrees to the ground.

POSITION 3 Now lower your right leg so that your right foot is back on the ground in its original starting position.

QUESTION 6

1	2	3	4	5
Very hard to see	Hard to see	Neither easy nor hard to see	Easy to see	Very easy to see

Enter your answer here: _____.

Question 7

Close your eyes and try to *feel* yourself performing the star jump without actually doing it. Rate the ease in which you could feel yourself performing this star jump on a scale of 1 to 5, with 5 being very easy to feel and 1 being very hard to feel.

POSITION 1 **Stand with your legs and feet hip-width apart and your arms by your side.**

POSITION 2 **Bend down slightly and then do a star jump into the air.**

POSITION 3 **Stand back in the original position.**

QUESTION 7

1	2	3	4	5
Very hard to feel	Hard to feel	Neither easy nor hard to feel	Easy to feel	Very easy to feel

Enter your answer here: _____.

Question 8

Close your eyes and try to *see* yourself moving your left leg and left arm out to the side without actually doing it. Rate the ease in which you could see your left leg and left arm move out to the side on a scale of 1 to 5, with 5 being very easy to see and 1 being very hard to see.

POSITION 1 **Stand with your legs and feet hip-width apart and your arms by your side.**

POSITION 2 **Raise your left leg and left arm out to the side.**

POSITION 3 **Now lower your left leg and arm back to the starting position.**

QUESTION 8

1	2	3	4	5
Very hard to see	Hard to see	Neither easy nor hard to see	Easy to see	Very easy to see

Enter your answer here: _____.

Scoring Table

After you have completed all the questions, you can enter your results into the table for the seeing imagery questions and the table for the feeling imagery questions. To get your total score for the seeing imagery questions, add up the scores for each question. For instance, if you scored 4 for question 1, 3 for question 3, 1 for question 6, and 2 for question 8, your total score would be $4 + 3 + 1 + 2 = 10$. Enter your scores in the seeing imagery question table (table 6.1) and then the feeling imagery table (table 6.2).

TABLE 6.1   Seeing Imagery Scoring Table

Question number	Answer
1.	
3.	
6.	
8.	
TOTAL SCORE FOR SEEING IMAGERY ABILITY: _____	

From A. Nicholls and J. Callard, 2012, *Focused for rugby* (Champaign, IL: Human Kinetics). Adapted from C.R. Hall and K.A. Martin, 1997, "Measuring movement imagery abilities: A revision of the Movement Imagery Questionnaire." *Journal of Mental Imagery* 21(1-2): 143-154.

TABLE 6.2   Feeling Imagery Scoring Table

Question number	Answer
2.	
4.	
5.	
7.	
TOTAL SCORE FOR FEELING IMAGERY ABILITY: _____	

From A. Nicholls and J. Callard, 2012, *Focused for rugby* (Champaign, IL: Human Kinetics). Adapted from C.R. Hall and K.A. Martin, 1997, "Measuring movement imagery abilities: A revision of the Movement Imagery Questionnaire." *Journal of Mental Imagery* 21(1-2): 143-154.

Understanding Your Scores

The total score that reflects your seeing mental imagery ability will range from 4 to 20. Likewise, your feeling mental imagery score will range from 4 to 20.

- **Scores ranging from 4 through 10.** If you scored between 4 and 10 on either seeing or feeling mental imagery, you struggled to see or feel the various images. As such, mental imagery will not benefit you as much as it would rugby players who have greater ability. But by practising imagery by recording your own imagery script (which is provided in this chapter) and then listening to your recording of the imagery script at least five times per week for a month, you can improve your imagery ability. The more your ability improves, the more of an effect mental imagery will have on your rugby performance. Complete the imagery questions again after a month to see whether you have improved. Do the same every month for six months to monitor your improvement.

- **Scores ranging from 11 through 15.** By scoring between 11 and 15 in either the seeing imagery questions or the feeling imagery questions, you are already fairly proficient at either visual or feeling imagery. Your rugby performance could benefit from mental imagery, and by practising mental imagery you will be able increase the benefits that it will have on your rugby performance. Make your own imagery CD by reading the script provided in this chapter and listen to it on a regular basis, at least five times per week, and then in the build-up to matches, such as the night before you play. Monitor whether your imagery ability has improved by completing the questionnaire on a monthly basis.

- **Scores ranging from 16 through 20.** Your score indicates that you are getting maximum benefits from using mental imagery. To maintain your current levels of mental imagery, you should continue to practise mental imagery. Use the script provided in this chapter to help you do this. Monitor your progress by completing the questionnaire to ensure that your imagery ability remains at this high level.

Note that you may have very different scores for your seeing imagery ability and your feeling imagery ability. If so, do not worry. When you practice imagining, try to improve the type of imagery in which you are weaker. For instance, if you scored 12 on seeing imagery questions and 4 on feeling imagery questions, spend more time trying to feel different images when you practice. Some people, no matter how much they practice, will always better at either seeing or feeling images. If you notice no improvement in your weaker form of imagery after several months, it might be best to stop practising that type of imagery. For instance, suppose that you initially have a seeing imagery score of 12 and a feeling imagery score of 4. If after three months of practising your feeling imagery score is still 4, it might be best to concentrate on improving your seeing imagery score.

Doing Mental Imagery

The easiest way to start using mental imagery is by using the imagery script provided in this chapter. Using this script will show you which types of images you should try to imagine and how long you should be imagining. Most mobile phones have the capability to record voices, so you can read the imagery script, record it, and then listen to it.

The imagery script provided is a generic imagery script that is suitable for all rugby players, but it is not performance specific. You can adapt and modify the imagery script for the position that you play. For instance, if you are a hooker you can change the imagery script to involve elements typical for that position, such as throwing the ball in at lineouts and scrummaging.

If you do not have access to voice-recording equipment, familiarise yourself with the imagery script by reading it several times and then spend about 10 minutes carrying out the different mental imagery exercises that you are asked to conduct.

Imagery Script

Get into a comfortable position and close your eyes. Focus on the centre of your body and take several slow deep breaths. With each inhalation imagine that you are pulling all the tension from your body into your lungs. With each exhalation, imagine that you are releasing all the tension and negative thoughts from your body. Continue this breathing, becoming more focused and confident.

Thirty-second pause.   Now imagine that you are about to perform a skill associated with playing your position such as [insert skill here—goal kick, lineout throw, lineout jump, catch high ball]. As you partially exhale, let your shoulders drop and arms relax. See yourself performing a [insert skill here—goal kick, lineout throw, lineout jump, catch high ball]. When you have exhaled to the point where you feel comfortable, perform your skill again in your mind but this time say your keywords "confident" and "focused" to yourself as you perform the skill. Besides seeing the skill, notice how your body is feeling. Notice how you feel what you would normally feel when performing this skill. Feel a sense of ease and lightness in imaging yourself performing this skill, almost as if performing this skill is effortless. Practice this skill in your mind again, saying your key words "confident" and "focused."

Thirty-second pause.   Now rehearse this skill several more times in various scenarios that would occur in matches. See and feel yourself successfully executing the task that you are imagining. Imagine that other players and coaches are present, but don't let them rush you. Notice how your concentration shifts from a broad focus as you are looking around to a narrow focus as you prepare to execute your skill. Imagine feeling that you have the ability to meet any challenges that you face. Spend some time practising your skill now as well as other skills associated with playing rugby and your position such as making tackles, passes, defensive formations, and attacking formations. Remember to say your keywords, "confident" and "focused," as you practice each skill for the next few minutes.

Three-minute pause.   Now imagine that you are about to perform a skill and are feeling a little tight. You want this one, and you start to worry about making a mistake. But you can stop your worrying by taking one breath. On the exhale say your keywords "confident" and "focused." Imagine the skill that you want to perform. You are confident and successfully recover by staying focused and in control of your emotions. Practice the skill now.

Twenty-second pause.   Now imagine yourself arriving at the ground feeling confident in both your mental and physical preparation, feeling good.

Twenty-second pause.   You feel the nervous anticipation of the competition and remind yourself that it is exhilarating to play rugby. You are motivated to perform.

Twenty-second pause.   You feel confident in your preparation and are clearly focused on your upcoming match. Your breathing is calm and controlled. Your muscles feel warm and elastic, ready to explode with intensity and precision. You are ready.

Twenty-second pause.   Your prematch warm-up goes well, and you remind yourself that you are ready for any unexpected obstacles. You are confident in your refocusing ability and remind yourself that you are mentally tough. You feel optimally energized and ready to go. Enjoy your match!

Getting the Most out of the Imagery Script

- Mentally imagery is a skill. As with all skills, good-quality practice will improve the influence that imagery has on your rugby performance.
- If you read out and record this imagery script, playing it back will take about 10 minutes, depending on how fast you speak.
- Remember to have the pauses in the script for the correct amount of time.
- During the first week listen to the recording of your imagery script twice a day. During the second week of your imagery training, listen to the imagery script once a day. After this, use the script the night before a match and on match day to prepare yourself mentally for matches.
- You can also listen to the imagery script before training sessions.
- Don't listen to the script whilst you are driving. You should have your eyes closed whilst listening to the script.

Four Ws of Imagery: Where, When, Why, and What

The four Ws of imagery are presented in table 6.3. Adhere to these principles to maximize the effects of imagery on your rugby.

TABLE 6.3   Four Ws of Mental Imagery

Four Ws of imagery	Answers
Where do you do imagery?	You can use imagery at home, at training, and at matches.
When do you do imagery?	You can use imagery before you go to bed on an evening; before, during, or after training; before, during, or after matches.
Why should you do imagery?	You can use imagery to practice a specific skill, help you relax, help you sleep, boost your confidence, increase your motivation, prepare yourself mentally for matches, and help you cope with injuries.
What do you imagine?	You can imagine everything that you would normally encounter when performing the specific skill in a real match including images, feeling in your body, noises, smells, and emotions.

THE MORE VIVID YOUR IMAGES ARE, THE MORE EFFECTIVE MENTAL IMAGERY WILL BE FOR YOU.

Summary

- Mental imagery refers to the process of using your imagination to see and feel yourself performing a particular movement.
- Using mental imagery can help improve your rugby performance, but don't expect immediate results.
- Images can be internal, in which you see the skill that you are performing from your own eyes, or they can be external, in which you see yourself performing the skill as though you were looking through a video camera and seeing your whole body. Either perspective is fine.
- The effects of imagery on your performance and emotional well-being depends on your ability, which you can measure and monitor over time. With mental imagery practice, your imagery ability should improve.
- Using an imagery script, such as the script provided in this chapter, allows you to structure your mental imagery practice sessions correctly.
- Make your images as vivid as possible. The more vivid and realistic your images are, the more of an effect they will have on your rugby performance.

CHAPTER 7

Building Confidence

I am not sure what happened. I was full of confidence and could do nothing wrong. Then I made a couple of mistakes in a match, and my confidence just vanished, almost instantly. I could not believe it. I was not sure how to get it back, nor did I understand why it had gone.

Stephen, current academy player

What Is Sport Confidence?

Sport confidence is the degree of certainty that you possess about your ability to be successful in sport. Sport confidence can be (*a*) general and represent your beliefs in always being successful (e.g., securing a professional contract, representing your country, or helping your team win the league) and (*b*) specific and refer to your ability to be successful in performing a task (e.g., tackling, passing, or kicking). Being confident at passing does not necessarily mean that you will be confident at tackling. Likewise, although you might be confident in your ability to be successful at rugby, you won't necessarily be confident in other areas of your life such as education, friends, or work.

False Confidence

Overconfidence does not exist. Confidence that is greater than actual ability should be termed false confidence. Rugby players or teams that have false confidence may experience a decline in their performance if they underprepare for a match because of their belief that they will easily win the match. That is, the confidence that people have in their ability does not match their true ability. A rugby player or team that has false confidence can experience a variety of undesirable consequences. For example, suppose that you are playing a team who is bottom of the league in your next match. You may be tempted to think that all you have to do is turn up and you will win. A consequence of this attitude or mind-set is that you might cut corners in training because you think that you don't have to work as hard. During the match, you might exert less physical and mental effort. In this instance, the confidence in your ability to be successful would be based on your usual level of preparation, but with less preparation or mental effort your performance will not be as good and you would have false confidence. Therefore, you must never take shortcuts in training or matches. Regardless of whether you are playing the team that is top of the league or bottom of the league, do not become a victim of false confidence by taking shortcuts in your preparation. Instead, earn the right to be confident.

Is confidence important in rugby? The answer is yes. Being confident in your rugby ability is important for a number of reasons. Sport psychology researchers have found that along with mental toughness, confidence is one of the most important characteristics in determining success in sport. The more confident you are in your ability, the better your performance will be. As a player you may have been supremely confident at times and experienced a drop in confidence at other times. Did you play better when you were more confident and worse when you were less confident? Take some time to think about the match in which you felt the most confident and the match in which you felt the least confident. Then complete table 7.1.

TABLE 7.1   Feelings of Confidence in Matches

Details and feelings	Felt most confident	Felt least confident
Opposition		
How did you feel?		
What specific aspects of your performance stood out (e.g., tackling, passing, kicking, or other)?		

From A. Nicholls and J. Callard, 2012, *Focused for rugby* (Champaign, IL: Human Kinetics).

Benefits of Being a Confident Rugby Player

A number of other benefits are associated with being confident.

- **Performance.** There is a positive relationship between sport confidence and performance. That is, people who are more confident perform better, whereas people who are not confident do not perform as well.

- **Emotions.** Research has revealed that the most confident athletes are able to remain confident and relaxed under pressurised situations during competition.

- **Concentration.** When you are confident in your ability, your mind is clear of worries about your ability to perform well, which allows you to concentrate on what you are doing, such as taking a goal kick or scrummaging.

- **Goals.** Confident athletes set themselves challenging goals and are more relentless in their desire to pursue such goals. Conversely, players who are not as confident do not set challenging goals nor are they as determined to succeed in achieving their goals.

- **Strategies.** Weinberg and Gould (2011) suggested there are two types of playing strategies: playing to win and playing not to lose. The most confident athletes have a play-to-win attitude, whereas less confident athletes play not to lose. A rugby player who adopts the play-to-win attitude always tries to make things happen, such as taking on an opponent in order to score a try, whereas a rugby player who has the attitude of playing not to lose looks for a pass rather than risks taking on an opponent and making a mistake.

- **Momentum.** Being able to reverse negative momentum created by circumstances such as losing four matches in a row or missing four kicks in a row is crucial in rugby. Confident players are able to reverse negative momentum by having a never-give-up attitude.

Callard the COACH

I know from my coaching experience that players all like individual confidence boosters before they play. Some even perform their confidence drills as late as the warm-up before the game. Whatever they do or whatever they want, you as a coach have to provide it! The players are the people who are about to take to the field, and they must feel prepared and full of confidence to tackle whatever comes in front of them.

Sources of Sport Confidence

The benefits of being confident are numerous, but you may want to know where your confidence comes from. Here is a list of factors that contribute to your sport confidence:

- **Mastery.** Developing and improving skills (but risk of losing confidence if you work on a particular skill, such as lineout throwing, and fail to perfect it).

- **Ability.** Demonstrating your ability by winning matches, outperforming your opponents, and outperforming your teammates.

- **Preparation.** Being prepared both mentally and physically for a match.

- **Self-presentation.** Feeling good about your body, weight, and overall appearance.

- **Social support.** Receiving encouragement from the people around you such as your coach and teammates as well as those outside rugby such as your parents and others (e.g., spouses, siblings, and friends).
- **Leadership.** Having faith in the leadership ability of the coach and the coach's decisions.
- **Other players.** Seeing other rugby players of similar abilities performing successfully in matches.
- **Environment.** Feeling comfortable in the environment in which you will perform; feeling comfortable among your teammates.
- **Situation.** Seeing breaks in matches going your way and having a feeling that everything is going be all right.

Callard the PLAYER

I always believed that sport confidence was linked to the work that you put into your game during the week leading up to a match. Situations would be acted out and various outcomes practised under pressure, both as an individual and as a team.

Individually, I covered a lot of outcomes. Of course, I could not cover them all, but I could cover those that mattered most to my position—kicking out of hand, taking high balls, and goal kicking. It was the foundation that I knew would underpin my performance! It was to be the launch pad from which my game could be effective for the team.

As a player for a number of years, I experienced a number of new training methods that became available. For example, overspeed training and using Rocket Ropes were the last things I did after my kicking on Friday before the game on Saturday. The training involved a series of sprints over 30 metres attached to a rope on a pulley system. The other person attached to the rope jogged in the other direction. Because the rope was on a pulley, the pull created in the other direction was three times as fast. As a result, you were pulled along at great speed and you had to maintain your form. Running so fast was a great confidence booster! Although I was not one of the quickest players, the training gave me a psychological edge in games.

Improving Your Confidence

You should recognize that a number of factors influence confidence and that building confidence takes time. Confidence can also disappear rapidly, so you should continue to engage in practice to maintain your confidence. For example, you might follow the recommendations that we outline to build your confidence and get results. If you fall back into your old behaviours, however, your confidence may disappear. To improve your confidence, adhere to the following recommendations.

Hard Work

Do not take any shortcuts in your training and preparation for matches. Earn the right to be confident through hard work. The following case study illustrates the importance of not taking shortcuts in training. This case study is based on a real example of a professional rugby union player who had just broken into the first team of his club.

CASE STUDY

Jim (pseudonym) is a 19-year-old professional rugby player who had played six games for his first team. He was a fly-half and experienced problems with his goal kicking during his third game. In his first two games Jim kicked well, but his performance had started to decline, as had his confidence. The following dialogue represents a snippet of the conversation that he had with his sport psychologist, who is referred to as SP.

SP: Jim, your coach tells me that you seem to have lost your confidence in recent games. I would like you to talk me through what has happened.

Jim: Yes, I have lost it, and I am not feeling confident at all. It all started when I played my third game for the first team. I kicked poorly, and the crowd really got to me. I could not stop thinking about whether I was going to get picked for the first team again because they had just signed another fly-half on loan.

SP: OK, let's go back in time slightly now. I want you to describe the first two games that you played for the firsts.

Jim: Well, they went well for me. I missed only three kicks in both of those matches together. I felt so assured about my kicking game that I knew I had a good chance of making every kick.

SP: How did that make you feel?

Jim: I felt brilliant. I felt good during the matches and felt good away from rugby, too. In the matches I wasn't thinking about anything other than kicking the ball through the middle of the posts. Even the kicks I missed went very close and were probably out of my range, but I told the captain I would have a go.

SP: You mentioned that your performance got worse in the third game. I was wondering if you did anything differently in preparation for your third game compared with you did for your first two games.

Jim: I had a tough week of training leading up to the third match because the coach wanted the players to improve their fitness. This has continued for the last few games, and I have not been putting as much time into my kicking after training. I have not been doing any extras.

In this case study, the player may have become a little complacent with his kicking after performing well in his first two matches, so he took shortcuts in training. He did not prepare fully, so his confidence suffered, as did his performance.

Be Rational About Success

Every player measure success differently. For instance, if you are currently playing for your club's fourth team and are then selected for your club's third-team squad, you have been successful. In table 7.2, list five things that you want to accomplish in rugby but make sure that they are achievable.

TABLE 7.2	What You Would Like to Accomplish in Rugby
1.	
2.	
3.	
4.	
5.	

From A. Nicholls and J. Callard, 2012, *Focused for rugby* (Champaign, IL: Human Kinetics).

Focus on Improvement

The most significant sport confidence that you can have is belief in your ability to get better at rugby. Don't judge yourself in relation to how other players are doing. Instead, focus on areas of your game in which you have improved and areas of your game in which you would like to improve. See chapter 2 on the performance profile for information about how to identify areas of your game that you would like to improve.

Develop Persistence

Regularly carry out position-specific practice in which you focus on specific elements of your game (e.g., lineout throwing, catching high balls, kicking, and so on). Developing these skills will set you apart from other players who play in your position. Ensure that you enter each training session with something that you want to practise and improve, such as your agility, strength, or kicking.

Mental Preparation

Prepare for all possible outcomes. Mentally prepare for optimal performance. Plan what you want to happen and visualise yourself being successful. For more information, see chapter 3 on preparation and chapter 6 on imagery. In addition, consider what could go wrong and work out how you will respond to it. That way, no surprises will occur during a match.

Self-Acceptance

Honour yourself no matter what and do not be too critical. If you have done the right things in the build-up to a match and given your all, then you have no need to be self-critical. Remember that you will always have another chance.

Physical Self-Presentation

Always display a confident demeanour, regardless of any mistakes that you make and especially after you make a mistake. Never reveal to your opponents that mistakes affect your confidence, even though internally it may have caused you stress. For instance, if a full back drops a high ball, his or her shoulders may drop. The player may look at the ground and display negative body language. The opposition team may then target that player. You should try to exude confidence at all times in these ways:

- Keep your shoulders pushed back. This action forces your chest and torso out. Your torso is vulnerable, but your posture demonstrates power and shows that you are not afraid of any confrontation.
- Always look straight ahead. If you make a mistake such as dropping a ball or giving away a penalty, do not look at the ground. Continue to look ahead and keep your chin up.
- Walk with a purpose during breaks in the game.
- Communicate clearly with teammates by maintaining the volume in which you would normally speak to them.

Sport the Library

Confident players like New Zealand's Sonny Bill Williams never let the opposition know what they are thinking and always appear to have a purpose, a posture that radiates power, and a look that isn't afraid of confrontation.

Callard the COACH

I like players to be honest, but I don't want to see them beat themselves up on the pitch. There is a right time and place for that, but it is not during a match. Some players go overboard and start remonstrating with themselves, physically showing the opposition that they are rattled. They must stay calm, realise their error, get over it, and live for the next pass they get or the next tackle they have to make.

Positive Self-Talk

No matter who you are, at times you have negative thoughts about yourself, which can reduce your confidence. You may think, *I am not good enough to be in this team* or *I am going to miss this kick*. Change negative thoughts that you may have into positive thoughts by using positive self-talk.

TASK **Write down negative thoughts which negatively affected your performance or confidence.**

This task will help you understand which situations have produced negative self-talk and why they produced negative self-talk. After you have done this, substitute the negative self-talk with an example of positive self-talk. To change a negative self-talk statement into an example of positive self-talk, you need to affirm

- your abilities,
- your skills,
- the training that you have been doing, and
- the preparation that you have done.

The example in table 7.3 illustrates how you can change negative self-talk into positive self-talk. Complete table 7.4 and change negative self-talk into positive self-talk.

TABLE 7.3   Changing Negative Self-Talk Into Positive
Self-Talk Example

Situation	Negative self-talk	Positive self-talk (changed into)
I missed a tackle in the first minute of the game.	"I am going to keep missing tackles because he is too quick."	"Every player misses a tackle at times. I'll concentrate on the next tackle and make sure that my technique is right."
I knocked the ball on.	"The coach is going to drop me."	"The ball was a little behind me. I will catch the next ball."
I missed five penalty kicks because of weather.	"I never kick well in the wind."	"Kicking will be hard for the other fly-half. I'll concentrate harder."
I was worried about playing against an opponent who had done well the last time we played.	"He is going to get the better of me again."	"I have improved since the last time we played. I'll continue doing what I have been doing and will perform better."
I was injured.	"I'll never get better from this injury."	"Recovering takes time. I'll get there in the end if I continue my rehabilitation."

TABLE 7.4   Changing Negative Self-Talk Into Positive Self-Talk

Situation	Negative self-talk	Positive self-talk (changed into)

(continued)

TABLE 7.4 *(continued)*

Situation	Negative self-talk	Positive self-talk (changed into)

From A. Nicholls and J. Callard, 2012, *Focused for rugby* (Champaign, IL: Human Kinetics).

Four Rs of Sport Confidence

R = Respond: Respond to any mistakes that you make in a match or in training by adopting a confident mind-set. You can do this by demonstrating confident body language and by focusing on what you will do next time that an opportunity arises in a game.

R = Respond: Respond with confidence to any criticism that you may receive from a coach, teammates, or the crowd.

R = Respond: Respond to problems by focusing on the solutions to solving the problem.

R = Respond: Refuse to accept a mediocre performance by preparing both physically and mentally.

Summary

- Sport confidence is the degree of certainty that you possess in your ability to be successful in sport.
- There is no such thing as overconfidence; we refer to confidence that is greater than actual ability as false confidence.
- The benefits of being confident include increased performance, enhanced emotional well-being, and better concentration.
- You can improve your confidence by not taking any shortcuts in your mental or physical preparation.
- Always exude positive body language during rugby.
- Use positive self-talk to boost confidence.

CHAPTER 8

Avoiding Choking

It was an important match. I knew that if we won we would secure promotion to the premiership, but I simply could not pass, kick, or catch the ball as well as I had all season. I was so tight it was unbelievable. In the last minute we made a break-away. I had two on one with the defender, and we needed the try, but I passed the ball forward and made a stupid mistake. I couldn't believe I had let my teammates down, but quite simply, I bottled it.

Lee, semiprofessional player

What Is Choking?

Choking in rugby occurs when you perform worse than you expect in relation to your skill level during an important match in which you experience pressure to perform. The desire to perform at your best in important matches (e.g., to win the cup, to avoid relegation, or to play well in front of selectors) causes performance pressure (Baumeister, 1984). The famous psychologist Sigmund Freud stated, "Many acts are most successfully carried out when they are not the object of particularly concentrated attention. . . . Mistakes may occur just on (those) occasions when one is most eager to be accurate" (1922, p. 23). In this quotation Freud is referring to the ease in which you may perform certain skills when there is no pressure or real concern about the outcome, such as in practice, and to the difficulty of performing the same skills when you particularly want to be successful, such as during an important match.

Choking generally occurs over a short time, such as from missing a kick at goal to missing several kicks at goal in an entire match. As such, choking has a clear beginning and end that you can easily distinguish (Beilock & Gray, 2007).

Callard the PLAYER

Every player dreads this happening and has no account of how or why it has happened. One minute you are standing over the ball thinking that you are one sweet swing from scoring the winning points, and the next you are wondering why you have snapped at it and sent it spiralling wide into the stand. Only with time will you get used to this and be in control of the situation.

Sport the Library

Choking is something that happens to most players and teams at some point, but applying psychology can help players like Argentina's Juan Fernandez Lobbe prevent it from affecting critical elements of their game, like kicking.

Nideffer (1992) suggested that a range of physical and psychological feelings are associated with choking, as outlined in table 8.1.

TABLE 8.1	Physical and Psychological Feelings Associated With Choking Under Pressure	

Physical feelings	Psychological feelings
Tight	Scared
Tense	Upset
Shaky	Panicked
Unsteady	Worried
Weak	Rushed
Heavy	Overloaded
Tired	Unsure

Why Do We Choke?

There is no definitive answer to why we choke under pressure, but psychologists have proposed two theories to explain the phenomenon, which are referred to as (1) the distraction hypothesis and (2) the explicit monitoring hypothesis.

1. Distraction hypothesis. The distraction hypothesis suggests that when you play in a high-pressure match you might experience worry. Your worry can distract you, which results in your being less focused on the task of taking a lineout throw, taking a goal kick, or making an important pass (Beilock & Gray, 2007). Consequently, your performance deteriorates.

2. Explicit monitoring hypothesis. The explicit monitoring hypothesis suggests that pressure causes you to (*a*) think about the movements that you make such as your leg action in a kick and (*b*) attempt to control the movements that you are making. Under normal circumstances you would not think about the movement in a kick nor attempt to control your movements, because you would perform the kick or other skill subconsciously (Baumeister, 1984). This monitoring and attempting to control movements disrupts the execution of the skill, which causes reduced performance (Beilock & Carr, 2001).

TASK Identifying Your Choking Experiences

To prevent choking from occurring, you need to recognise instances in rugby when you have choked (see table 8.2 for an example). Complete table 8.3 for a match in which you performed worse that you should have. Choking under pressure can be unpleasant, but you need to confront your choking experiences so that you can recognise the signs if you start underperforming in the future.

TABLE 8.2   Choking Under Pressure Experience Example

Match	Playing for my county last season
Why was the match important to you?	I knew that regional selectors were at the game, and I wanted to perform well in front of them. Also, it was my first game playing for my county, and I wanted to show everyone that I was good enough to play for the county side. It was an important game for me.
What happened?	The game went from bad to worse. I missed the first tackle I went for, and my lineout throwing was useless in that game. I kept throwing the ball waywardly, and my throwing distance was very poor. I threw a couple of balls too short, and I then started throwing the ball too long. I was substituted after 10 minutes of the second half, which made me feel even worse.
How did you feel physically?	Before the game and even up until my first missed tackle I felt physically strong and ready for the game. My preparation was good leading up to the match. But after that first missed tackle and poor lineout throw, I suddenly started feeling very tense. I could feel the tension in my shoulders and arms, especially as I was about to take a lineout throw. My arms felt really heavy, even though I had not done a weights session leading up to the match. I have never felt like that before.
How did you feel psychologically?	I was really worried, because this had never happened to me before. I was unsure about my ability as a rugby player, because I could not throw the ball in at lineouts. I knew that the regional selectors would not be impressed and that I had blown it. I also worried about what my parents were thinking, and I thought that I had let them down.

TABLE 8.3   Choking Under Pressure Experience

Match	
Why was the match important to you?	
What happened?	
How did you feel physically?	
How did you feel psychologically?	

From A. Nicholls and J. Callard, 2012, *Focused for rugby* (Champaign, IL: Human Kinetics).

Callard the PLAYER

A slight crosswind was blowing from left to right, but it was not enough to affect the flight of the ball and the kick at goal. My mental state, however, was not correct. I approached the ball off a shortened run up and stabbed the ball wide. I had actually strangled myself in the lead up to the kick by not giving it the respect it deserved. The team entrusted me with these duties, and I did not duly oblige. The incident taught me the valuable lesson that choking was just as likely to occur in a simple kick as it was in a difficult kick. I prepared fully every time after that. I applied a full preskill routine to every kick; no matter where it was on the field, it got my full attention.

Preventing Choking Under Pressure

Choking or performing poorly under pressure can happen to all of us, and it is not something to fear. In fact, choking under pressure is inevitable; all of us are likely to choke at some point in the future. Therefore, you should employ a number of strategies to recognise it and limit the effect that it has on your performance. Jordett (2010) identified a range of strategies, which are outlined in the following sections.

Preskill Routines

A preskill routine is often referred to a preperformance routine, but this term implies that the routine is carried out before the performance commences, such as in the changing room or on the coach to a match. We prefer to use the term *preskill routine*. A preskill routine refers to the sequence of thoughts (e.g., directing your focus to a target or blocking out any negative thoughts) and behaviours (e.g., staring at a target for a specific time or standing in particular position before taking a kick) that you use before performing a skill such as a kick, a catch from a restart, or a lineout throw. Recent research has found that developing and using a preskill routine can prevent you from choking (Mesagno, Marchant, & Morris, 2008). A preskill routine can prevent choking because it stops you from monitoring your movements when performing a specific skill.

Developing Your Individualised Preskill Routine

Research with basketball players from North America's National Basketball Association revealed that players were more successful in free-throw shooting when they followed their dominant preskill routine (Lonsdale & Tam, 2008). Because of the large positional variation in rugby and the different roles that each position is expected to perform, you should develop your own performance-specific preskill routine. You can do this by following the five steps outlined here.

Step 1 The first step in developing your preskill routine is to think about the skills crucial to your position in which you could use a preskill routine. These skills could include

- kicking the ball,
- lineout throwing,
- lineout jumping,
- catching a ball from the restart, and
- scrummaging.

If you perform any of these skills in rugby, then developing your own preskill routine could benefit you.

Step 2 After you have identified the skills crucial to your position, watch a player who plays in your position to see what he or she does. Your model could be an international player, professional club player, or amateur player. Closely examine the various behaviours that the player goes through on a consistent basis and note them in the table provided. Table 8.4 is an example of an international fly-half's preskill routine for goal-kicking attempts.

TABLE 8.4   Order of Behaviours in a Preskill Routine Example

SKILL: GOAL KICKING	
Order of behaviours	**Behaviour**
1	Checks the weather by throwing grass in the air and looking around
2	Looks at the post to identify the target
3	Bends down
4	Lines up the kicking tee
5	Puts the ball on the kicking tee and lines up the ball
6	Looks at the target once
7	Stands up
8	Looks at the target
9	Takes backward steps
10	Looks at the target again
11	Takes a deep breath
12	Looks at the target again
13	Initiates the goal kick

Depending on the skill relevant to your position, the player whom you chose to look at might not have as many behaviours in his or her preskill routine as the player in the example does. Preskill routines with fewer behaviours are not necessarily better or worse than preskill routines with more behaviours. The crucial element to a preshot routine in terms of preventing choking under pressure is consistency. Alternatively, the player whom you chose to look at may have more behaviours in his or her preskill routine. Watch a player who performs the skills a few times before writing down the behaviours included in his or her preskill routine in table 8.5.

TABLE 8.5   Order of Behaviours in a Preskill Routine

Order of behaviours	Behaviour
1	
2	
3	
4	
5	
6	
7	
8	
9	
10	
11	
12	
13	

From A. Nicholls and J. Callard, 2012, *Focused for rugby* (Champaign, IL: Human Kinetics).

In observing the preskill routine of a player you will realise that you can grasp only the behaviours of a routine, not the player's thoughts. Nevertheless, this chapter provides you with ideas on the thoughts that you could engage in during your preskill routine.

Step 3   You can create your own preskill routine by completing the preskill list. In this list you identify the point at which your routine will commence and then describe the sequence of behaviours and thoughts that you will engage in before completing the skill. An example of a complete preskill routine is presented in figure 8.1 on page 105. Remember that your routine is based on the order of behaviours that you listed in step 2 of this process.

You do not have to follow the same order as the person whom you observed because you might prefer to make your routine slightly different, which is fine. From the example in figure 8.1 you will see that we have included a variety of mental skills that you can use in you preskill routine such as mental imagery, thought stopping, or positive self-talk. All these skills are outlined in this book. Complete your own preskill routine diagram by completing figure 8.2 on page 106.

Step 4   After you have developed your preskill diagram, memorise the sequence of events that you listed. Then practice your preskill routine in a training session to see whether you think it will be feasible for matches. You should be able to use your preskill routine with ease and complete it with little if any thought. The routine should not distract you from performing the actual skill. When you first try your preskill routine you may become slightly distracted, which is normal, but this disruption should pass after several attempts.

Step 5   Step 5 is the most important step. You must use your preskill routine every time you perform the skill, whether in training or during matches. The more consistently you perform your preskill routine, the better your performance of the skill will be. You will also be less susceptible to choking under pressure.

Callard the COACH

As a coach you can help prevent choking from occurring by offering practices and sharing processes of the kick or throw with the player to help him or her develop a routine. The player should lead this exercise and not feel as if he or she is being subjected to another external pressure. Question the player and gather the responses to identify the critical triggers. In time the player will be self-reliant but initially will need guidance through the process of developing a routine.

Train With Anxiety

For some rugby players, the pressure to perform in certain matches may be a complete shock to the system and a cause of choking. Therefore, another way to alleviate choking is to ensure that anxiety is present when you train so that when you experience anxiety in matches you will be able to perform with this emotion present. You can create feelings of anxiety during training in several ways:

1. Adopt a mind-set that each training session is as important as matches that you will play. Although making a mistake in a training session is probably not going to be scrutinised in the same way that making a mistake in a match would be, you can increase your anxiety before training by thinking about the

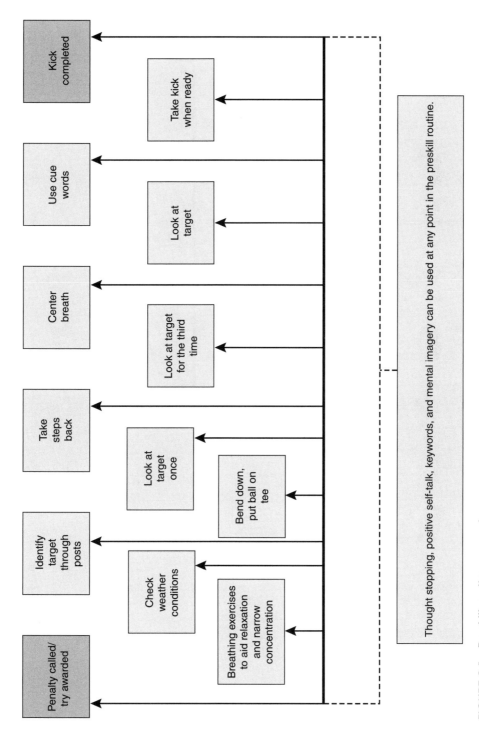

FIGURE 8.1   Preskill routine example.

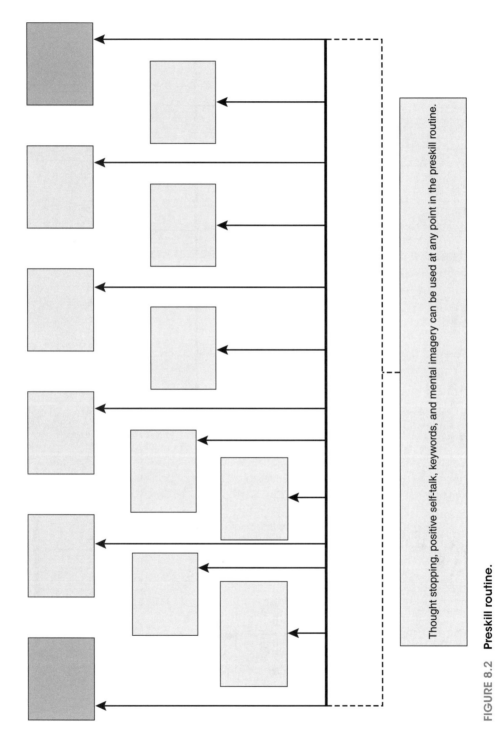

Thought stopping, positive self-talk, keywords, and mental imagery can be used at any point in the preskill routine.

FIGURE 8.2   Preskill routine.

From A. Nicholls and J. Callard, 2012, *Focused for rugby* (Champaign, IL: Human Kinetics).

consequences of a poor performance. Two consequences of training poorly could be losing your place in the team or having teammates develop a negative opinion of your skills. View everything that happens within a training session as being important.

2. Play games with yourself by setting targets. If you are practising a particular skill within training such as kicking or taking high catches, set a target of achieving a number of successful attempts before completing your training session. For example, if you are practising taking high catches, you might set yourself a target of taking 50 high catches in a row before ending your training session. Therefore, if you get to 49 high catches and drop the ball on the 50th attempt, you start again from zero. By the time you reach 40 successful catches in a row, you may experience some anxiety knowing that you will have to start again if you drop a catch.

3. Anxiety also has a physiological component, as outlined in chapter 5. Remember that anxiety is a stress emotion. The physical feelings of anxiety include an increased heart rate, muscle tension, some breathlessness, and increased blood pressure, to mention a few. These symptoms can be re-created by physical exertion. Therefore, if you are a lineout thrower you could physically exert yourself by performing some sprints and then immediately taking a lineout throw. By doing this you would be re-creating the instances in which you would be performing lineout throws in matches. Generally, you perform all skills in match settings under some physical duress, unless a particular skill such as a kick, scrum, or lineout throw is performed in the first minute of a match. Therefore, performing skills after some physical exertion has the benefit of re-creating some of the physical feelings associated with anxiety and making practice more closely simulate matches.

Increasing your anxiety during training will allow you to get used to playing well whilst experiencing anxiety. When you feel anxiety in training sessions, practice the coping skills and preskill routines that you would use in a match.

Monitor Your Movements During Training

Besides re-creating the feelings of anxiety associated with performing under pressure, athletes can mimic in training sessions the physical processes that occur during choking. Drawing from the explicit monitoring hypothesis, Beilock and Carr (2001) suggested that you can focus on movements whilst performing skills such as your leg action during kicking, your arm movement during a lineout throw, or your hand position when catching a ball in a lineout. By doing this you become more used to performing the skill when self-conscious, so that if this happens during high-pressure situations you will not choke.

Be Compassionate Toward Yourself

When players make mistakes they can be hard on themselves, a reaction often seen in rugby players when they drop a catch or miss a tackle. Some continue berating themselves for minutes, hours, or even days after the incident occurred. Leary (2004) suggested that you should accept that you are not perfect and that making mistakes in matches and losing are inevitable consequences of playing rugby. This idea is evident in the following quotation from a British and Irish Lions rugby union player:

> If you did not prepare yourself properly be angry at yourself. You may feel anger at other people when they make mistakes, but as soon as that comes in you think, *Whoa, people in glass houses.* You have got to account for 100 events in any rugby match, so at least 5 or 6 are going to go badly.

This quotation shows that the player has accepted that mistakes will happen. You must recognise that you will make mistakes, and when you do, you must forgive yourself. After you have made the mistake, focus on what you are going to do next, not the mistake itself. Besides being compassionate toward yourself, accept that everyone experiences negative emotions such as anxiety. After you learn to accept any negative emotions, your attention will not be diverted from the task that you are trying to complete (Jordett, 2010).

Summary

- Choking in rugby occurs when you perform much worse than you would expect to in relation to your skill level during an important match.
- Choking is something that generally occurs over a short time.
- Psychologists have proposed two theories to explain why we choke, which are referred to as (1) the distraction hypothesis and (2) the explicit monitoring hypothesis.
- Developing a preskill routine can prevent choking by ensuring that you direct your attention toward relevant things.
- Get used to anxiety in training so that you are not shocked when you experience this emotion during matches.
- Monitoring your movements whilst performing specific actions gets you used to performing skills self-consciously, so that if you tend to do this in a match you will not choke under pressure.
- Accept that you are going to make mistakes and be prepared to forgive yourself.

CHAPTER 9

Getting in the Zone

I felt great and just knew that no matter what I attempted in that game it would come off. I was in complete control of my game. In those 40 minutes nothing else seemed to matter.

Ben, professional player

What Is the Zone?

Rugby players often describe the instances when they have experienced peak performance as being "in the zone," but what exactly is this state? The zone refers to highly valued experiences in which you have felt completely at one with what you were doing on a rugby pitch. This might occur during the last 20 minutes of a match, or it could encompass the entirety of a match. When you are in the zone, you feel as though your performance is effortless. You have complete concentration and control over what you are doing, and you have an inner belief that you will be successful. Athletes use a number of terms to describe being in the zone, such as "in the bubble," "on auto-pilot," or "everything just clicking." The list is endless.

Callard the PLAYER

Although I have been in the zone many times whilst playing, I have never played a perfect game, nor has any team I have played on had a perfect game. Yes, we played good games, but never a perfect game! In the height of our supremacy when we were winning doubles, we used to say, "Strive for perfection knowing that perfection cannot be reached." We adopted this saying because no matter what we had just done, we knew we could always do better. Playing whilst in the zone would help us achieve this.

How Can You Experience the Zone More Often?

Emerging research suggests that you can do a range of things to experience the zone more often and more intensely, which has the potential to improve your performance. Before outlining how you can get into the zone more often, we will describe the zone. Sport psychology researchers agree that the zone consists of nine dimensions, which are listed here.

Skills-Challenge Balance

The element most required for you to experience the zone is having a balance between the challenge posed by the situation and your skills (Jackson, 1995). When you play a rugby match and don't believe that you are skilful enough to meet the challenge that your opponents pose, you may experience anxiety. On the other hand, when you think that your skills are too great for your opponents, you may experience boredom. Only when there is an optimal balance between the challenge of the situation and your skills will you experience the zone (see the shaded area in figure 9.1).

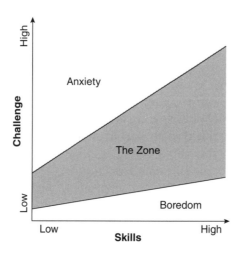

FIGURE 9.1   The skills-challenge balance.

TASK Identifying Your Own Skills and Challenges

Think of a time when you have played rugby and thought that (1) your skills were not sufficient enough to meet the challenge of your opponents, (2) your skills were far greater than the challenge that the opposition posed, and (3) your skills were equal to the challenge that your opponents posed. See table 9.1 for an example.

TABLE 9.1 Skills-Challenge Relationship in Rugby Example

Skills–challenge relationship	Situation	How did this make you feel?
1. Your skills were not sufficient to meet the challenge posed by your opponents.	Played a team two divisions above our team in the cup.	Really nervous, because we all knew we were going to be beaten.
2. Your skills were far greater than the challenge posed by your opponents.	Played the team bottom of the league who had not won a match all season.	A bit complacent. We all thought that if we turned up we would win.
3. Your skills were equal to the challenge posed by your opponents.	Played against our local rivals. The matches are always close because there is nothing between the two teams.	I felt really up for the match, because I knew it was going to be close, but if we played to our best we would win.

Now complete table 9.2 by providing as much information as possible. When completing the table, think of instances in which you felt anxiety or boredom. Have you played rugby when you thought that your skills weren't equal to the challenge?

TABLE 9.2 Skills-Challenge Relationship in Rugby

Skills–challenge relationship	Situation	How did this make you feel?
1. Your skills were not sufficient to meet the challenge posed by your opponents.		
2. Your skills were far greater than the challenge posed by your opponents.		
3. Your skills were equal to the challenge posed by your opponents.		

From A. Nicholls and J. Callard, 2012, *Focused for rugby* (Champaign, IL: Human Kinetics).

Action–Awareness Merging

When you are in the zone, action and awareness merge because of your total focus. You cease to be aware of yourself as separate from the action that you are performing (e.g., lineout throw), and you experience a feeling of oneness with the activity. You may also feel that your actions are effortless, spontaneous, and automatic.

Callard the PLAYER

When I was in the zone, kicking felt effortless—one smooth sweet swing with huge amounts of power and without a great deal of effort. I was striking them from everywhere with absolute ease. In fact, I had a shot from 52 yards straight in front. I tried to pinch a few yards whilst the referee turned his back; he caught me and marched me back to the original mark. I was so confident that I walked back five yards farther and struck it arrogantly through with plenty to spare. I was right in the zone, picking out the sweet spot of the ball with great accuracy.

Clear Goals

When you are in the zone you may have a clear sense of what you want to accomplish during rugby matches or training. As the event progresses so does the clarity of this moment-to-moment intent. You know exactly what you have to do and how you are going to do it.

Unambiguous Feedback

During zone experiences you often receive immediate and clear feedback. The feedback that you receive comes from what you are doing, such as where the balls are going when you pass or whether you complete tackles. Feedback also comes from your body, in particular your feelings during actions, such as the feeling in your leg during a goal kick. All feedback that you receive during zone experiences allows you to know how well you are doing. But feedback can come from multiple sources, such as coaches or teammates, and you should take every opportunity to make the most of any feedback that you receive.

Callard the PLAYER

I had full understanding of my goal-kicking mechanics. It was not purely the sight of the ball going through the posts that I judged my kicking performance on; it was also the feeling that I created through my sequence (that is, the flow of the kick), the sound that was made between the ball and the kicking foot, the shape of the ball in the air, and the speed at which the ball travelled through the air. All were critical factors in indicating the feeling of being in the zone. I knew instantly, because I had time in my head to analyse all these points.

TASK Indentifying Sources of Feedback

You need to be aware of the sources of feedback associated with optimal performances. Table 9.3 represents an example of some of the sources of feedback that you might have experienced (adapted from Jackson & Csikszentmihalyi, 1999).

TABLE 9.3   Sources of Feedback in Rugby Example

Source of feedback	Example
Awareness of bodily sensations	*Feelings of ease when running with the ball. It just felt fast.*
Visual information	*Seeing myself catch up with an opponent and then overtake him as we both chased the ball.*
Coach information	*Coach told me that I was playing well and to keep playing the way I was playing.*
Teammate information	*Teammates asked me to be narrower in the defensive formation.*
Outcome information	*I had not dropped a ball all game, so I knew I was doing well.*
Feel for correct skill	*Kicking out of my hand felt good. I just felt that the action was smooth, and I was kicking the sweet spot of the ball.*

You can increase your awareness of the sources of feedback by describing your own sources of feedback in table 9.4.

TABLE 9.4   Sources of Feedback in Rugby

Source of feedback	Example
Awareness of bodily sensations	
Visual information	
Coach information	
Teammate information	
Outcome information	
Feel for correct skill	

From A. Nicholls and J. Callard, 2012, *Focused for rugby* (Champaign, IL: Human Kinetics). Adapted, by permission, from S. Jackson and M. Csikszentmihalyi, 1999, *Flow in sports* (Champaign, IL: Human Kinetics), 97.

Concentration on the Task at Hand

When you are in the zone you will have a clear sense of focus regarding what you want to do. This feeling can last for several hours. Furthermore, when you experience this complete concentration you will be aware of other competitors and the bigger picture of what you have to do. But your awareness of your competitors will not be a negative influence because you will have complete concentration.

TASK   How Good Are You at Concentrating?

The grid in table 9.5 has been used to measure athletes' focus, and it shows you what complete concentration feels like. To complete the exercise, do the following:

1. Scan the grid for one minute.

2. Starting at zero, put a slash through as many sequential numbers as possible (e.g., 00, 01, 02, 03, 04, and so on).

3. Spend one minute slashing as many numbers as possible.

4. People who excel at concentrating are able to score between 20 and 30 numbers in a minute.

You can use the grid more than once by starting with a higher number than you did before, such as 50.

TABLE 9.5   Concentration Grid

32	42	39	34	99	19	84	44	03	77
37	97	92	18	90	53	04	72	51	65
95	40	33	86	45	81	67	13	59	58
69	78	57	68	87	05	79	15	28	36
09	26	62	89	91	47	52	61	64	29
00	60	75	02	22	08	74	17	16	12
76	25	48	71	70	83	06	49	41	07
10	31	98	96	11	63	56	66	50	24
20	01	54	46	82	14	38	23	73	94
43	88	85	30	21	27	80	3	35	55

Grid reprinted, by permission, from R.S. Weinberg and D. Gould, 2011, *Foundations of sport and exercise psychology,* 5th ed. (Champaign, IL: Human Kinetics), 391.

Icon Sports Media

When in the zone, players feel as if they're in a bubble. World champion fly-half Dan Carter illustrates this by being completely focused on the kick at hand.

Sense of Control

When you are in the zone you feel a complete sense of control without actually attempting to exert any control over what you are doing. You feel as though you can do nothing wrong, and you have a sense of invincibility. This sense of control frees you from the fear of failure and results in a sense of power, calmness, and confidence.

Loss of Self-Consciousness

Concern for yourself, worries, and negative thoughts disappear when you are in the zone. You will have no attention left to worry about the things in everyday life that may cause you to experience stress such as relationships, work, or education.

Transformation of Time

Some athletes have reported that time speeds up when they are in the zone, whereas others have said that time slows down and they think that they have a lot of time to make a decision. This element is the most controversial dimension of the zone because many athletes have never experienced it, nor could they relate to time speeding up or slowing down.

Autotelic Experience

When you get into the zone you find it extremely enjoyable, and all the tension and stress that you may have been experiencing before you started playing or training on a particular day disappears. When you are in the zone, you feel that you are on a complete high, which can last for several hours, long after you have finished your rugby match or training session.

Callard the PLAYER

When I analysed a moment in which I was truly in the zone, I knew it was not a one off. I regularly got into this state because I had practiced hard for it and had full comprehension of what I was looking for.

Getting Into The Zone More Often

Getting into the zone more often is desirable because being there is associated with optimal performance and maximum enjoyment. Using the recommendations proposed by Jackson and Csikszentmihalyi (1999), you can do a number of things to get into the zone more often during matches and training (see table 9.6).

Using the strategies presented in table 9.6 will help you experience the zone more often and more intensely. You can do a number of other things to help you enter the zone more often, and you should avoid doing some things that can prevent you from entering the zone. Russell (2001) and Jackson (1995) examined the factors that help athletes get into the zone and the factors that are likely to prevent them from getting into the zone. Nine factors can facilitate your getting into the zone:

Competitive plan   Previous experience

Optimal arousal   Focus

Motivated to perform   Optimal environment

Confidence and positive attitude   Performance feeling good

Optimal physical preparation   Positive team play and interaction

**TABLE 9.6   Strategies Associated With the Nine Dimensions
of the Zone**

Dimension	What you can do
Challenge–skills balance	See stressful rugby matches as being challenging. Identify what you can gain from each challenging match or training session (e.g., secure a professional contract, get selected for the national team, win the league, and so on).
	Set your own challenges before each match (e.g., make all your tackles).
	Enjoy the challenge that playing rugby brings.
	Believe in the practice and training that you have done, which will allow your skills to meet the rugby challenges that you face.
Action–awareness merging	Forget about yourself and don't worry about what others may think of you. Accept that mistakes will happen, but don't dwell on such mistakes.
Clear goals	Before each season, match, and competition, set some goals that you want to achieve. Work hard to achieve those goals.
Unambiguous feedback	Take advantage of all feedback that you receive.
Concentration on the task at hand	Focus only on what you want to do and how you will do it.
Sense of control	Do not strive for control. Work hard in training and let control come to you. It will just happen.
	Don't focus on the result of a match, the current score, or whether certain selectors are watching you. Focus on what you want to do.
Loss of self-consciousness	Let go of any worries and focus on the process of what you are doing, becoming completely immersed in what you are doing.
Transformation of time	If you experience a transformation of time, just go with it.
Autotelic experience	Always enjoy your rugby, whether you have won or lost.

To experience the zone more often, you should do the following:

- Develop a plan of what you are going to do during the competition in response to various scenarios. For instance, "If my opponent tries to side-step me, I will be ready to react and make the tackle."
- Know your optimal level of arousal. Are you the type of rugby player who performs better when you are psyched up, or do you play better when you are relaxed? If you play better when you are psyched up, increase your levels of arousal before competition. You can start by remembering previous

competitions when you were pumped. Alternatively, if you perform better when relaxed, stay away from teammates who like to psyche themselves up. Instead, engage in deep-breathing exercises.

- Enhance your motivation before competing by deciding what you want to achieve in the upcoming competition.
- Earn the right to be confident by preparing properly.
- Make sure that your training and diet leading up to the competition is correct.
- Use your experience by focusing on successful past achievements.
- Concentrate on what you want to do.
- Focus on the elements of your performance that have gone well.
- Interact positively with your teammates and encourage them.

Callard the **PLAYER**

Getting into the zone during matches was not just something that happened by chance, nor did it just happen overnight. I practised hard on my goal-kicking technique over many years to establish what worked for me. Thus, it was not a case of going straight into the zone; it was a case of establishing the zone—that being what I am looking for, what it should feel like, how it should sound—and then applying it in competition. Thus, in competition I knew what it was like to be in the zone because I had established what it felt like to get into the zone and what I had to do to get there, which was the transition stage before high-level competition.

Five factors make it less likely that you will experience the zone. You should be aware of these factors to minimise the likelihood of their occurrence.

- Not being physically ready or prepared for sporting competition will prevent you from getting into the zone. Therefore, you should establish precompetition routines that work for you and do them before every competition.
- Nonoptimal conditions such as noisy spectators or bad weather can prevent you from getting into the zone. You need to be able to block out spectator influence or poor weather.
- Athletes who lack confidence also struggle to experience getting into the zone. Prepare mentally and physically and take confidence from your preparation. Every time you start a rugby match, make sure that you have done everything possible to prepare.

- Inappropriate focus, such as focusing on the outcome of the competition, prevents you from getting into the zone. Focus on what you are doing and the actions required to enable you to attain your goals (e.g., body position during tackling).

- Poor precompetitive preparation can prevent you from getting into the zone. Sometimes problems that are not within your control (e.g., transport, opposition team arriving late, or poor facilities) can have a negative influence on your prematch preparation. If such things happen, make a conscious decision not to let them affect you. Refocus on what you want to do and how you are going to do it.

CASE STUDY

Earlier this year a 20-year-old fly-half, who was about to enter his second season as a full-time professional player, turned to his sport psychologist for some support. Paul (pseudonym) revealed that when he took kicks that he really wanted to make, such as when the scores were close or toward the end of a match, he had lots of negative thoughts in his head. He thought about what his teammates would think he if missed, whether the opposition fly-half would think that he was a good player, what his coaches would say after the game, and even what his parents would say to him after the game. All these negative thoughts occurred whilst he was putting the ball down and preparing to take the kick at goal. He said that at certain times, when he had kicked well, he had taken kicks without thinking too much and everything felt easy. Paul wanted to experience this feeling more often rather than have negative thoughts.

The role of the sport psychologist in this instance was to help Paul enter the zone more frequently. The first thing that Paul and his sport psychologist discussed was the negative thoughts that preoccupied Paul's mind whilst he was preparing for kicks at goal. In particular, Paul was questioned about the importance of other peoples' opinions about him as a rugby player. The sport psychologist asked questions such as "Does it really matter what Steve thinks about you?" and "Will your teammates, who are some of your best friends, think negatively if you miss a kick given the number of kicks you have made in previous matches?" These questions were asked so that Paul could start letting go of some of the negative thoughts caused by his preoccupation of what others thought about him.

Paul and the sport psychologist then spoke about what he would like to think about when kicking—in an ideal world. Paul said that he would like to think about the kick and nothing else. To help him with this, the sport psychologist encouraged Paul to focus on the process of kicking. They devised two key words: "head" (a reminder for Paul to keep his head down) and "leg" (a reminder for Paul to follow through). An imagery intervention was devised, which instructed Paul to imagine himself taking and being successful whilst taking kicks in challenging situations. Over time, after regularly practicing his imagery, Paul's negative thoughts became much less prominent. This process allowed Paul to get into the zone on a much more regular basis.

Summary

- The zone is a psychological state associated with superior sporting performance.
- The zone has nine dimensions.
- You can get into the zone more often by following the steps recommended in this chapter.
- Avoid the factors that prevent you from entering the zone.
- Enjoy being in the zone and the influence that it has on your performance.

CHAPTER 10

Managing Anger

I just lost it. I lost complete control for a few seconds and did not even think about getting sent off and letting my teammates down because they would have to play with only 14 men for (the) last 30 minutes. All I cared about was getting revenge on that player for what he had done.

Martin, retired professional player

What Is Anger?

Anger is an emotion that signifies a feeling of displeasure, which usually comes from fear (Hymans, 2009). Like all emotions, anger occurs for specific reasons. You can get angry toward other people when you think that they have committed a demeaning offence against you, whether that person is an opponent tackling you illegally off the ball, a coach not selecting you for a team, or a parent criticising your performance. Anger stems from the harm that the person has caused you or has the potential to cause you. You will probably also blame the person. For instance, you may currently be a club player who wants to represent your region. But if your coach does not pick you in your favoured position, he or she is harming your chances of playing at a higher level. Therefore, both harm and blame are present, so you could feel some anger.

Callard the COACH

Aggression and anger go side by side, and rugby players need a mixture of both, especially when competing for the ball at the breakdown or winning the collision in the tackle. The body needs to be fired up, and anger management is a large part of this.

Players get stoked up by fellow players and coaches alike as they try to raise their emotional state so that they can perform aggressively. I have seen players do some explosive lifting in the gym just before they play to increase their level of arousal. Others do some one-on-one contact skills to raise their arousal state.

Is Anger Bad?

Assuming that anger is either good or bad is a mistake. Anger is neither good nor bad, and it should not be classified as such because it can be both (Harbin, 2000). A negative consequence of your not being able to control anger is that you could commit an illegal or violent behaviour that could lead to your being sin-binned or sent off. Either way, you have let your teammates down, so you must not let your anger get out of control.

Anger can be useful, however, and you would not want to live your life without any anger at all. Anger is energy, so it can motivate you to try harder in a match or training session. When you get angry, you can also feel stronger, which has its uses when playing rugby. Essentially, anger can give you drive (Harbin, 2000) but only if you are able to control your anger and not let it control you. If you think that there have been instances whilst playing rugby or in your personal life when you have not been able to control your anger, then learning to control your anger could be of some benefit to you. To do this, you need to become aware of your anger and the consequences of being angry.

Callard the COACH

The best sides in the world have a great mix of ability with aggression and a good deal of anger in their play. You only have to watch them fire in to rucks with no backward step to see exactly what an angered controlled player looks like. They also run hard and at pace when carrying the ball, thus making themselves harder to bring down. We must remember that the game is about the hard yards in attack, and they have to be worked for.

A fine line separates being aggressive from being a dirty player, but the best players in the world know where that line is and rarely go across it.

Will You Still Be the Same Player if You Learn to Control Your Anger?

Commentators and coaches are perpetuating a myth when they say things such as, "If you take the anger out of the player, he will not be the same player." We do not believe this. As we said at the start of this chapter, anger can be used positively if it is controlled. Consider a player who focuses on seeking revenge against other players. This player's attention will be diverted from playing rugby, and he or she could spend time being sin-binned and suspended. If this player learned to direct his or her anger and the energy thus generated purely toward playing rugby, he or she would not be distracted by thoughts of gaining revenge on other players and would spend more time on the pitch. Would this make the player poorer? We don't think so.

ABCs of Anger

Anger has an antecedent or a cause. Think about the settings or scenarios in which you have become angry and have reacted with angry behaviour. In particular, focus on the events that occurred immediately before your behaviour occurred. Anger can influence our behaviour. As with all behaviours, consequences come with angry behaviour, which can be seen by viewing table 10.1 on page 124.

Write down the ABCs of your anger in table 10.2 on page 125. Think of the times when you have been angry. List the antecedents, your behaviour, and finally the consequences of your behaviour.

Anger Cycle

To control your anger, you need to understand the phases that occur in an angry episode. Arnett (1987) suggested that anger includes five phases, which are outlined in figure 10.1 on page 125.

Phase 1: Antecedents   The situation that you are engaged in starts stirring your emotions, leading to negative thoughts and feelings. A situation that provokes your feelings could be an opponent who breaks the rules.

Phase 2: Escalation   During the escalation phase your body is preparing physically for a fight-or-flight response. Because of evolution, when we feel threatened we are programmed either to fight what is happening or to run away, which is referred to as flight. Either way, the response is an adrenalin surge within your body; your muscles become tense, and your breathing may increase.

Phase 3: Crisis   During the crisis phase you are not able to make any rational judgements about what you are doing or are going to do, nor do you have any empathy for those around you.

TABLE 10.1   ABCs of Anger Example

Antecedents (cause) of your anger	Behaviour	Consequence
I was about to receive the ball when an opposition player hit me in the face.	I lashed out at other players and lost control.	When I was hit in the face, a mass fight occurred. I ended up getting my jaw broken, which resulted in a lengthy spell on the sidelines.
An opposition player put in a late tackle.	I started punching him whilst we were lying on the floor and did not stop even when the referee tried to stop me.	I was sent off.
My coach told me off in front of other players.	I lost my temper. I had a point to make, but the way in which I tried to make the point was wrong. In the end I started shouting at him and ended up walking away.	The relationship with my coach suffered, and I ended up not getting back in the team for another month.
A player cheated.	I ran after him so that I could get him.	The opposition team was awarded a penalty that resulted in their kicking for touch and then scoring from a drive after the lineout.
The referee made a silly mistake.	I tried to argue my point	The referee advanced their penalty 10 metres.
We lost in the semifinal of the cup.	I was very moody with my teammates. I did not talk to them after the match.	I am sure that they thought less of me after the way I behaved.

Phase 4: Recovery Your anger begins to diminish in the recovery phase. Physiologically, your body is starting to return to normal. Your adrenalin level is going down, your muscles are relaxing, and your breathing is becoming slower. But you are also primed to get angry if another incident occurs.

Phase 5: Restoration You are much calmer in this phase and may start to reflect on your behaviour. In particular, you may even start feeling guilty for what you have done.

TABLE 10.2 ABCs of Anger		
Antecedents (cause) of your anger	Behaviour	Consequence

From A. Nicholls and J. Callard, 2012, *Focused for rugby* (Champaign, IL: Human Kinetics).

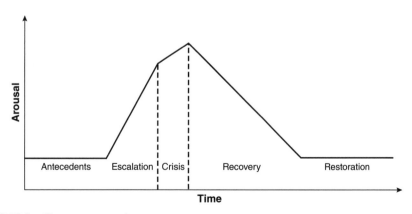

FIGURE 10.1   **The anger cycle.**

From M. Hymans, 2009, *Whole-school strategies for anger management: Practical materials for senior managers, teachers, and support staff* (London: Teach to Inspire). Adapted by permission of Speechmark Publishing Ltd. (www.speechmark.net).

Three-Step Approach to Taking Advantage of Your Anger

By reading this chapter you are accepting that you may have excessive anger, which could be ruining your rugby and indeed your personal life. To make a start on not letting your anger ruin your rugby, you can use the three-step approach (Harbin, 2000).

Step 1 If people have said that you have problems controlling your anger or if you have been sent off on many occasions, the first thing that you need to do before reading the rest of this chapter is to stop denying that you have a problem with your anger and the behaviour that you commit when you get angry. Denial is not a good way of dealing with any anger issues because you are ignoring reality. By being in denial you will never deal with your anger and the consequences of being angry.

Step 2 After you have stopped denying that you have problems controlling your anger, you are ready to take control and use anger to your advantage. You should make a promise to yourself to do your best to control your anger.

Step 3 Accept that controlling your anger will not be easy. Setbacks will occur, and improvements will not take place immediately.

Firework Model of Anger

Researchers have developed a firework model of anger to show you how anger works and, more important, to show you how to control your anger before it gets out of control (Faupel, Herrick, & Sharp, 1998). Imagine the three components of a firecracker as the stages of anger: (1) match, (2) body of firework, and (3) fuse.

1. **Match.** The match is the person, situation, and words that provoke or set off an angry response in you.
2. **Body of firework.** The body of the firework is your reaction both inwardly and outwardly to events.
3. **Fuse.** The fuse is your thoughts about what is going on.

Table 10.3 represents an example of antecedents, thoughts, and body reactions in situations when a person has experienced anger.

In table 10.4 on page 128, list situations in matches that you have played in the past against a rival team that provoked an angry response. Consider your thoughts at the time and your body reactions. This step is crucial in identifying the warning signs that you are becoming angry.

Now identify the reasons why each of the antecedents that you listed in table 10.4 causes you to feel angry. An example is presented in table 10.5 on page 128.

Write the antecedents of your anger from table 10.4 in the same order and list the reasons why you become angry in table 10.6 on page 129. Remember to be as specific as possible regarding what it is about each antecedent that makes you angry. Only when you have accepted and understood why you become angry about certain antecedents can you control your anger.

TABLE 10.3   Antecedents, Thoughts, and Reactions to Anger Example

Antecedents	Thoughts	Body reactions
Cheating	I am annoyed because I want the referee to see it. If the referee does not see it, I want to get revenge on the player.	It feels as though my chest is on fire. I can feel my heart pounding.
Crowd	I hate it when I can hear people in the crowd saying that I am no good.	I start feeling a little tense and nervous.
Coach	I don't think he rates me. I think I am better than my teammate, whom he picks more than me.	None really.
Parents	I think they wonder whether I try. Of course, I try my hardest, but things don't always go to plan.	I can feel anger welling up inside when they have a go at me sometimes.
Refereeing decisions	How can they be so incompetent to miss easy decisions?	My body feels on fire, and I have so much energy.
Cheap shots	I am frustrated that the referee does not see it.	My body feels pumped up and ready to retaliate.
Teammates making silly mistakes	I am annoyed that these mistakes might cost the team points.	It sometimes feels as though my body is going to boil over, especially if a mistake is made when we are about to score a try.

The antecedents may make you angry for a number of reasons. Some of the antecedents may make you angry because you think that they have the potential to humiliate you or make you look bad in front of other people. Alternatively, certain antecedents or situations may make you feel angry because you think that you are being taken advantage of or you are frustrated because people stop you from achieving important goals such as wining matches or being selected for a team (Harbin, 2000).

The common theme about feeling threatened, looking bad, being taken advantage, or having people prevent you from achieving your goals is that you perceive that a person or group of people are attacking you. The attack can be

TABLE 10.4 Antecedents, Thoughts, and Reactions to Anger

Antecedents	Thoughts	Body reactions

From A. Nicholls and J. Callard, 2012, *Focused for rugby* (Champaign, IL: Human Kinetics).

TABLE 10.5 Why Particular Antecedents Cause Anger Example

Antecedents	Why it causes anger
Cheating	When an opponent cheats I think that they are taking advantage of me and my teammates, which I don't like and don't think is fair.
Crowd	I think that the crowd is humiliating me, which makes me look bad in front of my family.
Coach	If the coach does not pick me, he is making me look bad and is stopping me from achieving what I want to achieve in rugby.
Parents	It causes anger in me because they sometimes think that I don't try, but I do. I sometimes get defensive and worry about what my dad will say next. I know that he means well, but I think he makes me feel embarrassed sometimes.
Refereeing decisions	If the referee makes bad decisions we are not going to win, and he or she has the power to stop my team from winning, especially if the game is close.
Cheap shots	If an opposition player takes a cheap shot and knocks me to the floor, I look bad in front of my teammates, coach, crowd, and parents. I don't like looking bad.
Teammates making mistakes	If teammates make mistakes they are stopping the team from winning. I know I make mistakes too, but I also feel angry when I make a mistake.

TABLE 10.6 Why Particular Antecedents Cause Anger

Antecedents	Why it causes anger

From A. Nicholls and J. Callard, 2012, *Focused for rugby* (Champaign, IL: Human Kinetics).

either physical or verbal. To control your anger, you must change the way that you think about certain anger-provoking antecedents. Our thoughts influence both actions and feelings, as outlined in figure 10.2.

Our actions influence the way that we think, and the way that we think influences our actions, so we must change the way that we think and the way that we intend to act when facing certain antecedents that may provoke anger.

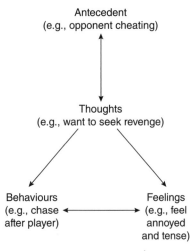

FIGURE 10.2 **Controlling your anger.**

From M. Hymans, 2009, *Whole-school strategies for anger management: Practical materials for senior managers, teachers, and support staff* (London: Teach to Inspire). Adapted by permission of Speechmark Publishing Ltd. (www.speechmark.net).

How to Manage Anger: Two-Part Process

The first phase of managing anger is accepting that you have an anger problem and then understanding what makes you angry and how you typically behave. The next stage of your anger management focuses on how to change your thoughts and modify your behaviours to beat anger.

Changing Your Thoughts

As a rugby player you will continue to face the antecedents that have caused your anger in the past. You cannot avoid situations in which opponents take cheap shots, referees make bad decisions, coaches do not select you for a team, or you receive criticism from the crowd.

We do not want you to lose your anger completely because as we said earlier, anger can energise you. But you should not lose control of your anger and commit behaviours that you will later regret because they are harmful to your team. Therefore, when you start to feel angry, instead of thinking about what you will do to an opponent or thinking that you have been hard done to, think about how you are going channel your extra energy and aggression. For example, an opponent may make a late tackle on you. Instead of thinking about taking revenge and risking being sin-binned or sent off, focus your thoughts on making your next tackle a big tackle, so that you use your extra energy legitimately to the benefit of your team. By doing this, you are not letting your opponents have a negative influence on your game. Instead, you are controlling your own destiny. So as soon as the feelings that you identified with being angry occur, focus on the behaviours that you are going to engage in.

Changing Your Behaviours When Angry

Besides changing your thoughts regarding the causes of your anger, you need to change your behaviour. Committing destructive behaviours may lead to your being suspended or getting injured, which can cost your team dearly, so you should use your additional energy legitimately. You can list the antecedents that cause you the most anger, the inappropriate behaviours that you have committed when you have lost control, and the way that you would like to act when the same situation occurs in the future. An example of antecedents, inappropriate behaviours, and ideal responses and behaviour is presented in table 10.7. You can complete your own list in table 10.8 on page 132.

When an incident occurs and you start feeling angry, immediately think about how you can channel your anger in a positive fashion and then behave in a way that takes advantage of the energy generated by becoming angry. By doing this you are not letting anger get in the way of your becoming the best player you can be. You will be focused on your own game and will spend more time on the pitch.

TABLE 10.7 Inappropriate and Ideal Responses to Anger Example

Antecedent	Inappropriate behaviours that you have committed in the past when you have lost control of your anger	How you would like to behave in the future
Cheating	Punched opponent	Channel energy into the next involvement in the game, whether that is a tackle, run, or high catch. Make sure that I focus on my role and stay within the laws of the game.
Crowd	Told them to shut up	Ignore the crowd and focus on my own game and what I have to do.
Coach	Argued with him	Try to understand the coach's point of view, listen, and then work on elements of my game.
Parents	Ignored them	Speak to them without shouting so that I can explain my point of view.
Refereeing decisions	Argued with the referee	Accept that arguing with referees is pointless, because they never change their mind after they have made a decision. Use my frustration positively in my next involvement in the game.
Cheap shots	Punched opponents	Do the same as what I said in relation to an opponent's cheating. I will channel all my energy and focus into my next involvement in the game.
Teammates making mistakes	Shouted at teammates	Instead of shouting at them and berating them, I will encourage them, which may increase the mood of the team and help them relax more. I will say something like, "Don't worry, you will get it right next time!"

TABLE 10.8 Inappropriate and Ideal Responses to Anger

Antecedent	Inappropriate behaviours that you have committed in the past when you have lost control of your anger	How you would like to behave in the future

From A. Nicholls and J. Callard, 2012, *Focused for rugby* (Champaign, IL: Human Kinetics).

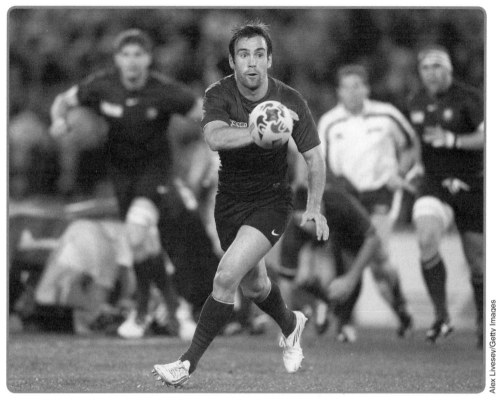

Even though he can be fierce on the field, France's Morgan Parra doesn't let anger affect his speed and keen vision in the heat of a play.

Alex Livesey/Getty Images

Summary

- Anger is an emotion that occurs when you think that a demeaning or unjust offence has been committed against you.
- Anger is negative if you do not control it.
- Anger can be positive if you use the energy that you gain from being angry in a positive manner.
- Change the way that you think and behave when you become angry.
- Focus on what you can do to make the most of the extra energy that you have from being angry in a positive manner and then execute the behaviour.
- Use anger to your advantage.

CHAPTER 11

Responding to Injury and Undergoing Rehabilitation

I heard the snap in my Achilles, and I knew it was going to be a bad one. All I could think about was that I was going to miss the World Cup and that I probably would not be around for the next one. I was completely devastated.

Jane, international player

What Is an Injury?

Kerr et al. (2008) defined an injury as an incident that occurs during a match or training that requires medical attention and stops you from playing rugby for at least one day after the injury occurs. Regardless of the level at which you play, you likely have already had an injury that has prevented you from playing rugby. Getting injured can be stressful, as revealed by the statement of a former British and Irish Lion international player:

> Probably the most stressful times are when you are in the middle of a nip-and-tuck game and you get injured. There is that initial few minutes of wondering whether you can battle on with this, whether you can still do your job at 70 percent. When you realise that it is a no, you are walking off the pitch and you don't want to look round at the boys because you feel you have let them down. You feel you have let everyone down so much. Injuries are unavoidable and they are just part of the game, but that is the hardest thing to deal with. A couple of years ago we were nip and tuck with the All Blacks, and I went off with about five or six minutes to go. We ended up losing by a point or two. I was captain at the time, and it was really disappointing. As a captain you want to lead from the front, and you almost take an injury as they have got one over on you, broken one of your players, which was pretty stressful.

Why Is Your Mental Approach to Injuries Important?

Although you can make a full physical recovery in that the stability, strength, stamina, and flexibility of the injured area may be the same as they were before the injury, psychological barriers may prevent you from getting back to your best. Psychological barriers can occur because of an injury or because of poor psychological rehabilitation during an injury (Taylor & Taylor, 1997).

Why Do Injuries Happen?

You might expect that physical factors such as overtraining, muscle imbalances, fatigue, and fitness are the main causes of injury. Research suggests, however, that psychological factors also play a role. For instance, stress levels have been identified as a major factor in causing injuries. That is, athletes who have the most stress in their lives experience more injuries (Williams & Andersen, 1998).

The relationship between stress and injury rates baffled sport psychologists for a number of years. Evidence suggests that athletes who have lots of stress in their life get injured more often, but what is the explanation for this relationship? Two theories have been presented to explain it:

1. Attentional disruption. When we experience stress our attention becomes hampered, as does our peripheral vision, which means that we can see

David Jones/PA Wire/Press Association Images

Ireland's Brian O'Driscoll has had more than his share of setbacks but has continued to come back a stronger player by rehabbing both mind and body.

less of what is happening in a rugby match. If you are experiencing stress in your life, your vision may be narrowed and you may fail to see a tackle coming. Therefore, you do not brace yourself for the tackle (Williams, Tonyman, & Andersen, 1991).

2. Increased muscle tension. When you experience stress your muscles are more tense, which interferes with coordination. Your tackling might not be as accurate, which can result in your getting injured (Smith, Ptacek, & Patterson 2000).

Psychological Responses to Injury

Injured athletes tend to go through three distinct phases in response to an injury. The speed and ease at which people go through the three phases can vary dramatically, depending on a number of factors such as personality, the injury sustained, and the rehabilitation process. The three phases are referred to as the injury information-processing phase, the emotional upheaval phase, and the positive outlook phase (Udry, 1997).

Injury Information Processing   After the injury has occurred you focus on information such as how much pain the injury is causing you, how long the injury will keep you out of rugby, how the injury happened, and what you could have done differently to prevent the injury from occurring. You may also start to recognise the consequences of the injury, such as missing important matches or even missing the enjoyment of training and being around your teammates.

Emotional Upheaval   After you have become aware of how long you will not be able to play, you may experience a range of negative emotions such as anger, agitation, and frustration. You may also be emotionally depleted, feel isolated from your teammates, have feelings of self-pity, or be in denial about the injury.

Positive Outlook   You accept the injury and deal with it. Your mood becomes elevated and optimistic, and you are relieved as you see progressions in your rehabilitation.

Callard the COACH

When a player had an injury, especially a long-term injury, I would meet with him to discuss the injury, to let the player know that he was still in my thoughts despite his being out for eight or nine months. I would get the player involved in match analysis or coaching the junior rugby players. I wanted to get the player involved as much as possible and let him know that he was investing time in himself and for the good of club. It is a partnership! It is vital that players be involved whilst they are injured.

Rehabilitation

After your injury has been diagnosed you will start a phase of rehabilitation. The length of the rehabilitation depends on the injury and can vary from a week to several years in extreme cases. The purpose of rehabilitation is to enable you to repair the injured part of your body so that you can compete again. During your rehabilitation you may spend a long time working on restoring the injured parts of your body. Besides doing this physical rehabilitation, you need to engage in mental rehabilitation so that you experience emotional well-being during your time away from rugby and do not face psychological barriers on your return. Part of the mental rehabilitation involves understanding some of the negative feelings that you may have during rehabilitation and making an effort to overcome such negative emotions. According to Taylor and Taylor (1997) rehabilitation comprises four stages.

Stage 1: Range of Motion   The primary goal of this stage of the rehabilitation process is to increase the range of motion of the injured area. In this stage of rehabilitation you are likely to experience pain because you will be performing movements that are unfamiliar and beyond your control. You therefore need to engage in pain management strategies. Advice on pain management is provided later in this chapter.

Stage 2: Strength   After you have 80 percent range of motion in your injured body part, you are in stage 2 of the rehabilitation process. You will now begin to start testing the injured area for the first time since your injury. You may have some doubt about the ability of your injured area to manage the demands placed on it by testing it out. This apprehension can lead to cognitive anxiety (worry or nervousness) and somatic anxiety (muscle tension, breathing difficulties, or increased heart rate). Advice on managing anxiety during the rehabilitation process is offered later in this chapter.

Stage 3: Coordination   After your strength has improved significantly, you enter what Taylor and Taylor (1997) referred to as stage 3. In stage 3 you continue strength training, but the training is more specific in that it includes movement patterns that build balance, agility, acceleration, and speed in the injured area. You need to maintain positive focus during this stage, because as the exercises that you do more closely simulate matches, you will inevitably make comparisons about how good you used to be. At this stage the comparisons will not be favourable, so you must maintain a positive focus.

Stage 4: Return to Sport   The final phase that completes the rehabilitation phase occurs when you return to sport. At this stage the injured area will be at its preinjury level, so physically you are ready to start competing again.

Setbacks During Rehabilitation

The four stages outlined by Taylor and Taylor (1997) may give the impression that rehabilitation is a relatively straightforward process, whereby you go from one phase to the next with relative ease and make constant progress. This ideal progression will not always happen, and you may experience setbacks along the way. Most rugby players believe that rehabilitation is a steady process, but this does not always occur, as outlined in figure 11.1.

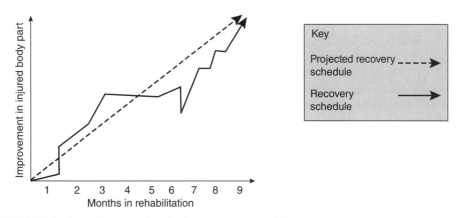

FIGURE 11.1 **Perceived and actual recovery schedule.**

Adapted from J. Taylor and S. Taylor, 1997, *Psychological approaches to sports injury rehabilitation* (Gaithersburg, MD: Aspen Publishers).

Recovering from injury is not a steady process, as highlighted in the actual recovery graph. Recovery is an unstable experience that includes ups and downs, setbacks, and plateaus when you do not see any improvements for some time. You need to understand that the recovery process and healing take time.

Responding to Setbacks During Rehabilitation

Experiencing a setback may elicit a range of feelings such as worry, frustration, anxiety, or even depression. But such setbacks can serve a specific function in the recovery phase. They provide you and your medical staff with information on the healing process and the speed of the rehabilitation program that you are undertaking. Accepting setbacks as part of the healing process is vital.

Fear of Rest During Rehabilitation

Injured athletes, especially those who are highly motivated and disciplined, may struggle to understand that rest is crucial in the rehabilitation process because it boosts recovery (Kindermann, 1988). If the medical professionals tell you to rest, you can do so without feeling guilty. Rest is just as important as the physical regime (Taylor & Taylor, 1997).

Callard the PLAYER

I was flying! Everything was going well. The training with the club, the personal training, and the matches were proving to be both enjoyable and successful. The team was gaining some identity for good rugby, and the part I was playing within it was very fulfilling. Then it struck, like a shot out of the blue—a pulled hamstring. The frustration and anger that I experienced were enormous. Everything was going so well, and then suddenly everything stopped.

I felt like this partly out of anguish, because I had worked hard to establish myself in the side and was contributing to it. Second, I was frustrated because I did not have the release of exercise that I had become used to. But this was only the beginning. I forced treatment and overdosed on inappropriate exercise that later caused problems. When I felt that the hamstring was responding well, I abused it and was set back, not only from playing but also from training, both club training and personal training. The downward spiral began again, and this time I was a little more angry and a little more frustrated.

Through time I got through it, purely through good fortune because there were natural breaks in the playing programme, which allowed me to relax in the sense that I was not in the side and not part of the team. Only when I looked back on the situation and the anguish that I had caused to those around me did I understand what I needed to do in the future.

I needed to apportion blame, even just for self -gratitude. I blamed myself or other players, but I eventually accepted that the injury was in the past. The only thing that I could control, which is what I subsequently did with later injuries, was to accept that I was injured and that my participation levels would be lowered. Thus, I needed to concentrate on what was required for the future and the role I had to play in that from a physical and mental perspective.

A detailed plan was drawn up that noted frequency of treatments, frequency of tests, and a progressive monitoring system that allowed me to progress from one stage of rehabilitation to the next. An example of this was a simple uphill walking session on the treadmill for 20 minutes. If I completed this session pain free with full range of movement, I could move to the next stage, which was to do some straight-line running over various distances without sudden stopping. Physically, I had satisfied myself, but more important, I felt good psychologically knowing that I had completed the programme correctly and that I was making progress.

Also important in my process of dealing with the injury was understanding what the injury was, how it happened, and what was needed to correct it. This was fascinating, because it was almost a picture in my head of where I needed to go—what the three-centimetre tear actually looked like, how it repairs itself, and what it looked like when it was in a semirepaired state. I could better understand the consequences of my actions if I chose not to follow the prescribed rehabilitation course.

Psychological Strategies During the Rehabilitation Process

You can use a range of strategies to manage the feelings that you are likely to encounter during rehabilitation. Strategies such as goal setting, rehabilitation profiling, mental imagery, and coping that have been discussed in detail in other chapters can be used to deal with injuries in much the same way that you would use them to improve your game.

Goal-Setting Staircase

Setting goals is crucial to enhancing your motivation and adherence, and it is vital when you are injured. The staircase method is an example of how you can set a range of progressive goals. You may want to complete this exercise with your physiotherapist or doctor. Figure 11.2 is an example of a goal staircase.

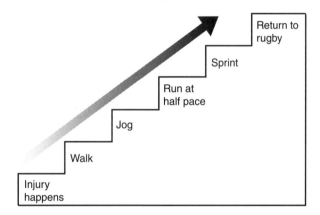

FIGURE 11.2 **Goal-setting staircase example.**

After the injury happened, this player first intends to walk, jog, run at half pace, sprint, and then return to rugby.

When setting your goals, make sure that they adhere to the SMARTER goals principles outlined in chapter 1. Complete the goal-setting staircase in figure 11.3.

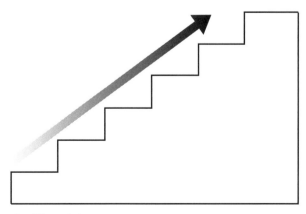

FIGURE 11.3 **Goal-setting staircase.**

From A. Nicholls and J. Callard, 2012, *Focused for rugby* (Champaign, IL: Human Kinetics).

Rugby players often just set the goal of returning to their sport injury free. This simple approach is fine, but if you adopt it you might be missing the chance to improve areas of your game that you normally don't have time to work on. For example, if you know that you will be unable to play for several months because of a knee injury, you have the opportunity to work on other aspects of your physicality, such as your upper-body strength. You could therefore set yourself a goal of returning to rugby stronger and faster than you were before the injury. Table 11.1 can help you identify your weaknesses before you were injured and then set goals for when you return to rugby.

TABLE 11.1   Returning to Rugby After Injury Example

Weaknesses preinjury	Goal for your return to rugby
Speed	To improve my 30-metre sprint time by 0.2 seconds
Strength	To bench press 80 kg
Agility	To run the shuttle run in 35 seconds
Fitness	To improve my fitness by getting to level 15 of the bleep test

Complete table 11.2 to identify your weaknesses before you were injured and the areas that you would like to improve when you make your return to rugby. If you are unsure about your weaknesses or the parts of your game that you should work on, talk with your coach. In addition, always speak to your medical professional to ensure that you can safely work on the areas that you have chosen.

TABLE 11.2   Returning to Rugby After Injury

Weaknesses preinjury	Goal for your return to rugby

From A. Nicholls and J. Callard, 2012, *Focused for rugby* (Champaign, IL: Human Kinetics).

Rehabilitation Profiling

This strategy uses the same premise as the performance profile does, but it is aimed toward the rehabilitation process. As such, rehabilitation profiling focuses on the physical and psychological factors that are crucial throughout the rehabilitation process. Table 11.3 is an example of a completed rehabilitation profile.

TABLE 11.3	Crucial Physical and Psychological Factors During Rehabilitation Example	
Physical		**Psychological**
Coordination		Focus
Stability		Motivation
Balance		Expectations
Swelling		Confidence
Pain		Worries
Health		Being able to take the pain of rehab
Sleep		Persistence
Range of motion		Attitude
Strength		Commitment

Phase 1: Identifying Physical and Psychological Qualities   Write down the qualities that you believe are crucial to recovering from your injury in table 11.4. Consider both physical and psychological qualities. These represent a range of likely contributory factors to success in your rehabilitation. Try to generate as many qualities as you can.

TABLE 11.4	Crucial Physical and Psychological Factors During Rehabilitation	
Physical		**Psychological**

From A. Nicholls and J. Callard, 2012, *Focused for rugby* (Champaign, IL: Human Kinetics).

Phase 2: Selecting the Most Important Qualities and Defining Their Meaning After you have listed the most important physical and psychological factors, you should define what each quality means to you. Phase 2 of the performance profile involves your listing the most important qualities from phase 1 and then writing down what each quality means to you. An example generated from table 11.3 is presented in table 11.5.

TABLE 11.5   Meanings Associated With the Most Vital Factors in Rehabilitation Example

Quality	Meaning
Balance	Being able to put weight on my leg
Motivation	Being up for doing all the rehabilitation
Persistence	Not giving up
Coordination	Getting movement back
Stability	Feeling strong at joint
Range of motion	Having freedom to move my leg
Attitude	Being positive
Commitment	Not shirking rehabilitation
Sleep	Getting good rest
Focus	Not being distracted during rehab
Being able to take pain	Accepting the pain that I will have to take
Worries	Not worrying about lack of progress

Review the qualities that you listed in table 11.4 relating to physical and psychological qualities that are important in the rehabilitation process. Write them down in table 11.6 and describe what they mean to you.

TABLE 11.6   Meanings Associated With the Most Vital Factors in Rehabilitation

Quality	Meaning

From A. Nicholls and J. Callard, 2012, *Focused for rugby* (Champaign, IL: Human Kinetics).

Phase 3: Plotting the Rehabilitation Profile   During this phase you list the qualities and then rate yourself on a scale of 1 to 10 by colouring the appropriate boxes. An important point to consider is what a score of 10 actually means. Assume that 10 is your maximum potential score. After you have completed the performance profile, prioritise what you are going to improve in the action point box. In addition, state in specific terms how you will be able make improvements. See figure 11.4 on page 146 for an example of a completed profile. Then complete your own rehabilitation profile in figure 11.5 on page 147.

Date _____	Ratings									
Quality	**1**	**2**	**3**	**4**	**5**	**6**	**7**	**8**	**9**	**10**
Balance	▓	▓								
Motivation	▓	▓	▓	▓	▓	▓	▓			
Persistence	▓	▓	▓							
Coordination	▓	▓	▓	▓	▓	▓	▓	▓	▓	
Range of motion	▓	▓	▓	▓						
Stability	▓	▓	▓	▓	▓					
Attitude	▓	▓	▓	▓	▓					
Commitment	▓	▓	▓	▓	▓	▓	▓			
Sleep	▓	▓	▓							
Focus	▓	▓	▓	▓	▓	▓				
Being able to take the pain of rehabilitation	▓	▓	▓							
Worries	▓	▓	▓	▓	▓					

Action points

-
-
-
-

FIGURE 11.4 Rehabilitation profile example.

Date ______________________	Ratings									
Quality	**1**	**2**	**3**	**4**	**5**	**6**	**7**	**8**	**9**	**10**

Action points

-
-
-
-

FIGURE 11.5 **Rehabilitation profile.**

From A. Nicholls and J. Callard, 2012, *Focused for rugby* (Champaign, IL: Human Kinetics).

Mental Imagery

Chapter 6 outlined how you can use mental imagery to develop strategies for playing at your best. Research suggests that mental imagery can not only improve performance but also aid recovery (Durso-Cupal, 1996). It is thought that imagery promotes healing of the injury by increasing blood flow and warmth to the injured area (Blakeslee, 1980). Imagery can serve a number of other purposes when you are injured such as replacing the physical practice that you are no longer able to do with mental practice, allowing you to see yourself recovering, mentally practicing skills that you learned before your injury, and controlling negative disturbances that can be associated with being injured.

To promote healing, you can imagine images associated with the healing process such as

- blood flowing to the injured area,
- ice on the injured area blocking out all pain,
- the injured body part performing movements, and
- the injured body part feeling strong.

You can use imagery during actual rehabilitation sessions or in the privacy of your home. Spend at least 10 minutes per day doing healing imagery. With regard to the performance-orientated mental imagery that you can do whilst injured, see the imagery script in chapter 6 (page 84) and use it to create your own imagery script. You could adapt the instructions to imagine yourself recovering from the injury or controlling the negative emotions that you might be experiencing whilst injured.

Coping

Like goal setting, profiling, and mental imagery, coping was discussed earlier in the book. Being injured and going through rehabilitation can be stressful, so you have to cope with the stress that you experience. Recent research with a sample of professional rugby union players suggested that avoidance is an effective coping strategy when dealing with a long-term injury, such an anterior cruciate ligament injury (Carson & Polman, 2010). The two types of avoidance coping are behavioural avoidance and cognitive avoidance.

- **Behavioural avoidance.** Coping strategies classified as behavioural avoidance involve you physically removing yourself from a stressful situation, such as by walking away from a coach who is shouting at you.
- **Cognitive avoidance.** Coping strategies classed as cognitive avoidance involve attempts to disengage mentally from thoughts surrounding a stressor, such as blocking out the pain of an injury.

The research by Carson and Polman (2010) reported that several behavioural avoidance (see table 11.7) and cognitive avoidance strategies (see table 11.8) were effective. When you are injured try using these coping strategies to manage any stress that you may encounter during your time away from rugby.

TABLE 11.7   Effective Behavioural Avoidance Strategies

Effective behavioural avoidance coping strategies for managing long-term injuries	Example
Take up a new hobby	Learn a new language
Involve self around team	Do match analysis for team or scout opponents
Continue outside interests	Learn new recipes
Organise coaching sessions	Coach younger players at your club

TABLE 11.8   Effective Cognitive Avoidance Strategies

Effective cognitive avoidance coping strategies for managing long-term injuries	Example
Denial	When in painful rehabilitation sessions, deny that you are experiencing pain by blocking out the thoughts of pain.
Change conversation to a subject other than injury	Quite often people may want to talk about your injury, but you may not. If you don't want to talk about your injury, change the subject to something that you are comfortable talking about.

Managing Pain During Rehabilitation

Rehabilitation sessions can be extremely painful, so you must use a range of strategies to manage the pain that you encounter. Two of the most popular techniques to manage pain nonpharmacologically are abdominal breathing and dissociation.

Abdominal Breathing

According to Taylor and Taylor (1997) this method is the simplest and one of the most neglected ways of reducing pain. To heal more effectively and reduce pain, the body needs a greater amount of oxygen than normal, which can be gained through long, slow inhalations associated with abdominal breathing. To do this type of breathing,

1. lie on a cushioned floor or on your bed with your hands clasped on your lower abdomen,
2. inhale through your nose to the count of 4, and
3. exhale slowly to the count of 5.

Dissociation

Dissociation involves directing your attention away from the pain that you are experiencing. You can distract yourself internally by counting, by imagining yourself being on your favourite beach, by humming a song, or externally by listening to music, by watching television, or by reading a book.

You can use abdominal breathing or dissociation during rehabilitation sessions or when you are at home and need some pain relief. Try the various methods and see which works for you the best.

Positive Focus

To help you maintain a positive attitude during your injury period, you can focus on the four Ps (Taylor and Taylor, 1997):

- **Positive.** Think about the positive features of your rehabilitation.
- **Present.** Think about the present and don't look too far ahead or dwell on the past.
- **Process.** Think about what you need to do daily to enhance your recovery.
- **Progress.** Think about the gains that you have made.

Returning to Play

After you have completed your physical recovery you will be ready to resume playing rugby, which can be both physically and emotionally demanding. The challenge will be in proportion to the length of time that you were injured and the severity of your injury. On your return to competitive action, you may have doubts that you will ever be able to return to the level at which you were playing before your injury, which is normal. Taylor and Taylor (1997) stated that when you return to competitive rugby you will go through five stages: (1) initial return, (2) recovery confirmation, (3) return of physical and technical abilities, (4) high-intensity training, and (5) return to competition. Having an understanding of these phases will ease the transition to full competition.

1. Initial Return   Stage 1 of this five-stage process involves your initial return to training with your teammates. This process can be demanding psychologically because you will find out how successful your rehabilitation was. You may also be excited because you will be playing rugby again after what may have been a long time away from the game. But people tend to develop unrealistic expectations, which may lead to disappointment. You may expect in your return to rugby that your rehabilitated injury will be free of pain and that you will be able to perform as you did before the injury. If you have some pain and decreased performance you could become worried and down. Finally, some rugby players may be concerned about the rate of their progression and push themselves faster than it is safe to do. Be realistic in your expectations and discuss any concerns that you have with your physiotherapist or doctor.

2. Recovery Confirmation   During this stage you receive confirmation either that your injury has healed or that there may be complications. A successful initial return to training will provide you with evidence that your rehabilitation was effective, which will have a positive effect on your confidence and motivation. But if your return to training is not successful you may experience physical difficulties such as unexpected pain, swelling, decreased strength, and compensation injuries to other parts of your body. You may also experience a range of psychological difficulties because you may start thinking that all your rehabilitation efforts were wasted.

3. Return of Physical and Technical Abilities   During this stage you start to increase the intensity of your training to improve your conditioning, and you can spend time practicing the technical skills associated with your position that you have not been able to practice whilst you have been injured (e.g., passing, kicking, catching, and so on).

4. High-Intensity Training   You can now take part in high-intensity training to improve your conditioning, and you can do contact work so that you become used to physical contact again. All aspects of your injured area should be better or the same as they were before you sustained your injury.

5. Return to Competition   After you have improved your physical conditioning you will be ready to return to competitive action. You may feel excited at being able to play rugby again because all your hard work during rehabilitation is going to be rewarded, but you may also feel nervous. If you feel nervous, use the coping strategies outlined in chapter 5.

Fear of Reinjury

Although you have healed physically, you may experience psychological stress from the injury on your return to competitive play (Taylor & Taylor, 1997). The fear of being reinjured may cause the most stress (Heil, 1993). A fear of being reinjured can cause psychological difficulties such as reduced focus and decreased confidence, as well as physical difficulties such as muscle tension. These complications increase the likelihood that you will become injured again.

Fear of injury can occur from spending time away from your sport and being isolated whilst being injured. If you spend a long time away from the rugby environment, you will lose contact with the sport and thus have less familiarity and control on your return. Therefore, you should try to maintain involvement in some way during the time when you are injured. You could do match analysis, scout opponents, or even run some coaching sessions. This additional education might be beneficial when you return to rugby (Taylor & Taylor, 1997).

Despite your efforts to stay involved with your team, you may still have concerns about getting injured again. This fear may arise when you are about to resume training or about to make your return to competitive rugby. If this occurs, you should recognize that being apprehensive is normal. These fears will likely pass with time.

To accelerate the rate at which your fear of reinjury disappears, you should establish the cause of your fear. Any number of circumstances could prompt your fear, such as being in a situation in which your injury occurred (e.g., being tackled), returning to the same venue, or even not wanting to go through a bout of rehabilitation again. After you have established the cause or causes of your fear, you should challenge your fear of injury. You can do this by testing your injured body part and measuring how strong it is. When tests confirm that this part of your body is strong enough, you know that you are ready for the rigors of rugby. Take confidence and trust from this finding and let the fear go.

Summary

- Psychological factors such as stress in your life can increase the likelihood that you will get injured.
- When you get injured you go through three phases: the information-processing phase, the emotional upheaval phase, and the positive outlook phase.
- When you get injured identify the areas that you would like to make stronger than they were before your injury.
- Besides doing physical rehabilitation for your injury, you can use a range of psychological skills to help ease the rehabilitation process, such as rehabilitation profiling, goal setting, and coping.
- Don't be too concerned by setbacks that occur during rehabilitation. Accept that this is part of being injured.
- Stay involved whilst you are injured by scouting opponents, doing match analysis, or running some coaching sessions.

CHAPTER 12

Using Progressive Muscular Relaxation

I used to be too tense, especially on match days, and I think it affected my performance. Tensing and relaxing my muscles really helped me relax, and I felt energised going into the games.

Andrew, county rugby union player

What Is Progressive Muscular Relaxation?

Progressive muscular relaxation, also known as PMR, refers to the process of tensing and then relaxing your muscles. This technique can help you deal with the physical symptoms of stress such as (*a*) overtensed muscles before playing, (*b*) as a postmatch recovery aid when your body is aching, and (*c*) as a sleep aid if you are having problems sleeping. If your muscles are too tight on match days, you could do PMR on the morning of a match, the night of a match, during a training session to aid recovery, and when you are trying to go to sleep if you are having problems sleeping. The technique is called progressive muscular relaxation because you are tensing and then relaxing various muscle groups within your body until all your muscles are completely relaxed. The purpose of PMR is to relax your muscles, which in turn can relax your mind.

What Does PMR Involve and How Long Does It Take?

PMR involves your tensing various muscle groups for about 7 seconds and then relaxing the same muscles for 30 seconds, based on the instructions that you receive. In total, each PMR session will last about 20 minutes.

What Are the Benefits of PMR?

PMR offers a number of benefits. First, by tensing and relaxing your muscles you become aware of the difference between when your muscles are tense and when they are relaxed. You are then able to detect tension in your body and eliminate it. This point may seem obvious, but without being able to detect muscular tension you cannot work to get rid of it. When you become proficient at PMR you will automatically detect muscle tension and then be able to release any tension that will interfere with your performance (Williams & Harris, 2001). Second, by directing blood toward the muscles, PMR aids muscle recovery by reducing the aches and pains that result from a match.

Callard the COACH

Postmatch progressive muscular relaxation techniques are a must for the modern player. Anything that can aid recovery after a heavy training session or game has to be incorporated into the rugby programme. Initially, PMR might be done as a group, but ultimately, responsibility is in the hands of the individual players.

How Can You Do PMR?

In this chapter we provide you with a PMR relaxation script. You can read this script, record it to your smart phone, and play it back. Alternatively, you can become familiar with the instructions and do the exercises yourself. The most effective way is to record the script and play it back to yourself.

Where Can You Do PMR?

You can do PMR anywhere that is quiet and comfortable, such as in your bedroom, whilst travelling to a match on the bus, or whilst sitting in a parked car. Changing rooms are not the most suitable place to engage in a 20-minute PMR session because they are too noisy and distracting.

How Often Should You Do PMR?

There is no definitive answer to this question. You can do PMR as much or as little as you think necessary. If you go through a time when you experience lots of muscle tension and stress, you might benefit from doing two 20-minute PMR sessions per day.

When Should You Do PMR?

You should do PMR whenever you feel the need to relax or whenever you experience muscle tension. This need will vary from player to player; some players may experience tension the night before a match, whereas others may experience it the morning of a match. Think about the times when you usually experience muscle tension and plan to practice PMR during or right after those times.

Additionally, research with a sample of professional rugby union players found that muscle aches and pains were the worst on the day after matches as opposed to on match day or the day before a match. Therefore, conducting a PMR session on the night of match or the day after a match might help reduce such muscle aches. Try this yourself to see whether you notice any difference.

PMR Script

When you record the script onto a Dictaphone or mobile phone, please ensure that you leave the required pauses in the script. These pauses allow you time to release the tension from the muscles. Before starting your PMR session, you should be seated in a comfortable position in a quiet and private place.

You will be asked to tense and then relax 16 separate muscle groups: approximately 5 seconds for larger muscle groups and 3 seconds for smaller muscle groups. You will then be asked to relax for 20 seconds. Do not start tensing until you have been given the instruction tense. Continue your tensing until you are told to relax. As soon as you hear the word *relax*, release all tension in that muscle.

Lie in a comfortable position and close both of your eyes. You will start by tensing the muscles in your legs and then move up your body to your trunk, then arms, shoulders, neck, and face. Tense the muscles in your right calf muscle. That's good. Feel the tension in your right calf.

Pause for 5 seconds. Relax.

Pause for 20 seconds. Tense the muscles in your right thigh.

Pause for 5 seconds. Relax.

Pause for 20 seconds. Your right leg should be feeling nice and relaxed now. Now move on to your left leg. Tense the muscles in your left calf muscle. That's good. Feel the tension in your left calf.

Pause for 5 seconds. Relax.

Pause for 20 seconds. Now tense the muscles in your left thigh.

Pause for 5 seconds. And now relax.

Pause for 20 seconds. Both of your legs should be feeling nice and relaxed. You will now start work on your trunk and upper body. Now tense your abdominal muscles.

Pause for 5 seconds. And now relax.

Pause for 20 seconds. Good. That feeling of relaxation should be spreading up your body. Now tense your pectoral muscles.

Pause for 5 seconds. Relax.

Pause for 20 seconds. That's good. Feel the relaxation spread up your body. Now tense your shoulders by pushing against the surface you are lying on.

Pause for 5 seconds. Relax.

Pause for 20 seconds. That is excellent. Your legs and upper body should be really relaxed. You will now work on relaxing your arms, starting with your right arm. Tense the muscles in your right forearms. That's good. Feel the tension in your forearm.

Pause for 5 seconds. Relax.

Pause for 20 seconds. Now tense the muscles in your right biceps.

Pause for 5 seconds. Relax.

Pause for 20 seconds. The whole of your right arm is now feeling nice and relaxed. You will now move to your right arm. Tense the muscles in your left forearm. That's good. Feel the tension in your left forearm.

Pause for 5 seconds. Relax.

Pause for 20 seconds. Now tense the muscles in your left biceps.

Pause for 5 seconds. And now relax.

Pause for 20 seconds. Notice how both of your arms, along with your legs, trunk, and shoulders, are feeling nice and relaxed. You will finish with the neck and the facial muscles. Now tense your neck muscles by pushing your head gently against the surface you are lying on.

Pause for 5 seconds. And now relax.

Pause for 20 seconds. You will now finish by relaxing your facial muscles. Tense your jaw muscles by pulling an exaggerated smile.

Pause for 5 seconds. And now relax.

Pause for 20 seconds. Now tense your cheek muscles by pushing your lips out and squinting your eyes.

Pause for 5 seconds. And now relax.

Pause for 20 seconds. Finally, tense your forehead muscles by raising your eyebrows as high as you can.

Pause for 5 seconds. And now relax.

Pause for 20 seconds. That is excellent. Notice how relaxed your whole body feels. Enjoy this feeling of relaxation. Before finishing, scan your body to see if you have any remaining tension. Start with your left calf, then your left thigh, followed by your right calf and right thigh. If there is any tension, tense the muscle and then let it relax. Now scan your abdominals, followed by your chest, then shoulders. Again, if there is any tension, systematically tense and then relax the muscles. Finish by scanning your right forearm, right biceps, left forearm, left biceps, neck muscles, jaw muscles, cheek muscles, and forehead. You should now be enjoying this complete state of relaxation.

Now, spend a few moments enjoying this state of relaxation. [Pause for 1 minute.] That is excellent. Notice how your muscles feel refuelled and ready for anything. Before opening your eyes, take some deep breaths.

Inhale deeply to the count of four (1 . . . 2 . . . 3 . . . 4). Now exhale to the count of six (1 . . . 2 . . . 3 . . . 4 . . . 5 . . . 6). Inhale deeply to the count of four (1 . . . 2 . . . 3 . . . 4). Now exhale to the count of six (1 . . . 2 . . . 3 . . . 4 . . . 5 . . . 6). Inhale deeply to the count of four (1 . . . 2 . . . 3 . . . 4). Now exhale to the count of six (1 . . . 2 . . . 3 . . . 4 . . . 5 . . . 6). Inhale deeply to the count of four (1 . . . 2 . . . 3 . . . 4). Now exhale to the count of six (1 . . . 2 . . . 3 . . . 4 . . . 5 . . . 6).

That is excellent. Open your eyes.

Enjoy the feeling of your muscles being completely relaxed. Let all your muscles go limp as any remaining traces of tension drain out of your body. Scan your body, starting at your head and working your way down to your feet. If you notice any tension, tense that muscle for 7 seconds and relax for 30 seconds. You may feel a warm sensation throughout your body, or you may even feel as though you have sunk into the floor or into the chair that you are sitting on. Alternatively, you may feel very light, almost as though you could float away. Whatever you are feeling, enjoy being relaxed.

Before you open your eyes, take five deep breaths and allow energy and the feeling of alertness to flow through your body. Stretch your arms and then stretch your legs. Open your eyes.

Passive Muscular Relaxation

After you have become proficient in active and deep muscle relaxation through following the script presented in this chapter, you are ready to engage in passive muscular relaxation. With passive muscular relaxation you do not tense the muscles before relaxing them. Instead, you just let go of any tension present in that muscle. You follow the same procedure of sitting in a comfortable position, going through each muscle group, and then relaxing that muscle group. Relax your muscle groups in the following order:

1. Right hand and lower arm
2. Right biceps
3. Left hand and lower arm
4. Left biceps
5. Muscles in face—forehead, eyes, and mouth
6. Neck and shoulders
7. Abdomen and buttocks
8. Right thigh
9. Right foot, ankle, and calf
10. Left thigh
11. Left foot, ankle, and calf

Let all the tension drain out of each muscle group and enjoy the feeling of relaxation. This process will not take as long as PMR does, and you will find that you need less time to feel muscular relaxation as you get better.

Summary

- PMR refers to the process of tensing and then relaxing your muscles to achieve total muscular relaxation.
- PMR can help reduce muscle soreness after matches.
- PMR can be done whenever you feel muscular tension or are struggling to sleep.

CHAPTER 13

Overtraining and Underperforming

I was going into matches tired. I was doing too many extras after training and not giving my body time to recover. I was really run down. I was absolutely shattered by the start of the second half and really struggled to finish the game off.

Scott, premiership player

What Is Overtraining and the Unexplained Underperformance Syndrome?

One way of improving your performance is to undertake a more intense physical conditioning program so that you are able to perform at higher intensity for the whole 80 minutes of a match. Although increasing your training has the potential to achieve this, engaging in extra training can result in your experiencing physical stress (Polman & Houlan, 2004). If you are not able to deal with the stress from training, your performance may deteriorate. Any performance decline over a sustained time is termed the unexplained underperformance syndrome (UPS). Overtraining occurs when you engage in lots of training and do not get sufficient rest, which leads to reduced performance or UPS. As such, UPS is an outcome of overtraining.

The impact of overtraining can be highly detrimental to performance. When you are overtraining, your performance suffers during matches. You become fatigued much earlier in a match and find it harder to perform various skills as the match progresses. For instance, you might find that you miss more tackles because you don't have the energy to use the correct tackling technique or are not able to get to the player whom you want to tackle. Your passes might not find their target, or if you are kicker, you might make mistakes that you would not normally make.

Callard the COACH

It is easy for a player to get into a routine and have no progression in training. The player thus gains nothing from his or her training. Training can help a player either to get better technically or to perform well; the outcomes are different, and the training must be kept separate. Thus, when looking at the whole picture of the season, a player must plan for development and include in it different training phases or cycles. Otherwise, the season will be one cycle without any peaks.

Do Not Confuse Overtraining With Overreaching

Overreaching occurs when you train harder than normal. The result may be temporary feelings of fatigue and physical stress, but with adequate rest you are able to come back and perform better than you did previously. As such, the combination of training and rest allows you to reach your full potential. Overreaching is the first phase of overtraining, but with adequate rest and recovery whilst in a fatigued state, you can reverse the symptoms and recover within one or two weeks (Kuipers, 1998). With overtraining, performance may not return to previous levels for as long as several months, despite resting (Kreider, Fry, & O'Toole, 1998).

PAUL ELLIS/AFP/Getty Images

With overtraining, you risk causing yourself injury on the field that could sideline you from key games, like English fly-half Toby Flood did during the 2009-10 season.

What Are the Symptoms of Overtraining?

The clearest indicator that you may be in an overtrained state is that you are not able to perform at previous levels (Richardson, Andersen, & Morris, 2008) in either fitness tests (e.g., bleep test) or strength tests (e.g., one repetition max), or you just find yourself being extremely fatigued during matches when normally you would be able to play much longer before becoming fatigued. Generally, the symptoms of overtraining are much more severe than those of overreaching (Halson & Jeukendrup, 2004) and may include the following:

- Performance decline
- Mood disturbances, such as depression, anger, and confusion
- Decreased immune system, which results in more illnesses, allergic reactions, and upper respiratory tract infections (Armstrong & VanHeest, 2002)
- Muscle aches
- Lack of energy
- Sleep disturbances
- Appetite changes

Callard the COACH

Monitoring whether an athlete is underperforming is not the sole responsibility of the player. It should be a collective effort of the player, coach, fitness team, and medical team all working together. A coach should be able to spot a drop off in performance on the field.

Risk Factors Associated With Overtraining

Some research has examined the risk factors associated with symptoms of overtraining among a sample of professional rugby union players (Nicholls et al., in press). This paper found a number of risk factors associated with overtraining:

- Training (structure and volume)
- Number of matches and recovery period
- Diet
- Sleep
- Travel

The quotations in table 13.1 on page 162 reveal how the various risk factors may contribute to symptoms of overtraining such as decreased performance and mood disturbances.

TABLE 13.1 Risk Factors Associated With Overtraining Among Professional Rugby Union Players

Risk factor	Quotation from professional rugby player
Training	"It was the build-up of the whole week, and I felt dead and buried at the start of the season. My body was shaking and everything. We only got two days off—one day before a match and one day after a match at that time in the season. We were training full time down here, and some players were feeling a bit sore and stuff. I think during the game it affected my performance because I was feeling tired quicker instead of lasting the 80 minutes, and I was feeling it more in the second half rather than at the back end of the second half. I felt like I was getting more knocks and bruises and aches and pains after a game."
Number of matches played and recovery period	"I was down here [at the training ground] at 7:30 [a.m.]. I was tired anyway, did not know I had to play on the Wednesday, and got a text asking me to play. I wanted to say no, but when somebody says you are needed you don't want to let people down. I was quite fatigued and tired. I got down there, and he said I was starting, and I thought, 'Oh, God.' Muscle pains were so bad, as I had done a max session, finding out our maxes in the morning, and I just did squats and bench presses. My legs and arms were just gone. As a prop you need both legs and arms, so I was very tired. I had driven down there. I was not in the frame of mind. I was tired, lethargic, and didn't feel in the game."
Diet	"My tiredness comes from not eating regularly. So that is one of the things I'm looking at now because I have been feeling a bit tired. On match days I get up and have something really good to eat. I will be eating all the way through to the game, and I am also more rehydrated. . . . I came in, and I hadn't had any breakfast. I was feeling a bit hungry and dehydrated and did my weights session. Smashed it out on the weights and then went out on the field and was feeling a bit . . . I'm a bit knackered now."
Sleep	"I remember one night when I was very tired, and although I got to sleep OK and slept through the night, I had sort of that feeling where you feel you have not been to bed and wake up feeling tired. When you are tired or carrying knocks you just don't feel well. Although you are asleep you still feel as though you can feel them even when sleeping, and you feel tired the next day."
Travel	"It was a long journey with five hours on the bus that could have contributed to it [poor performance] as well. I have been suffering with my body like at the beginning of the season when I was fighting for my place. I was on the bench for the first team but still playing for the second team as well, so I was preparing for two games a week and spending a lot of time on buses travelling around Britain. That was not good for me and was really hard work."

Diagnosing Overtraining

No diagnostic tool is currently available to detect overtraining in rugby players. Rather, overtraining is diagnosed only when all other factors that may explain decreased performance (e.g., injury) or mood states (e.g., mental illness) are ruled out (Halson & Jeukendrup, 2004). Although there is now no way of diagnosing overtraining, you can monitor symptoms associated with overtraining such as stress and affective states. By monitoring your levels of stress you can change your training regime if your levels of stress are high or if you have negative affective states. Identifying problems early might be the key to preventing overtraining from occurring (Richardson et al., 2008).

Callard the COACH

Many top sporting clubs are adopting some simple measures to monitor players' welfare and whether they are in an overtrained state. These methods vary from the use of global positioning satellite systems to track players' movement in training sessions to simple wellness charts whereby players are asked to submit scores about how they are feeling. Questions asked relate to the amount of sleep they have had to their soreness or stiffness from the exertions of the previous day. The players' weight is recorded daily. Some clubs even conduct osmosis tests to determine whether a player is sufficiently hydrated. Players who are not hydrated are asked to consume fluids and may even be pulled from training to reduce the possibility of an injury.

A coach must not be frightened to act on the information gathered. After all, players must feel their best if they are to perform to their best.

A coach must be flexible. He or she must be prepared to change training, for the individual or for the whole group. The coach must plan rest weeks and encourage players to take time off during the season. Periodic rest will keep the players motivated, fresh, and enthused.

Players must also show honesty to spot signs of fatigue or training stress early on and be open about them. They must be prepared to take time off, change their training schedule, or have the discipline to take on new activities that are not physically draining.

Monitoring Stress

Rushall (1990) devised a questionnaire called Daily Analysis of Life Demands in Athletes (DALDA). We have adapted this questionnaire (see table 13.2 on page 164) and called it Daily Analysis of Life Demands in Rugby Players, which you can complete yourself. To monitor your stress levels, complete this questionnaire on a regular basis such as once a week or once a month. Part A of the questionnaire refers to sources of stress (e.g., diet, home life, and friends), and part B refers to symptoms of stress (e.g., muscle pains, temper, and likeability).

TABLE 13.2 Daily Analysis of Life Demands Among Rugby Players

INSTRUCTIONS: CONSIDER HOW YOU HAVE BEEN FEELING IN THE PREVIOUS WEEK AND CIRCLE THE APPROPRIATE RESPONSE ALONGSIDE EACH ITEM.

Part A: Sources of stress	A = worse than normal	B = normal	C = better than normal
1. Diet (e.g., whether you're eating regularly with adequate amounts)	A	B	C
2. Home life (e.g., whether you're arguing with your family)	A	B	C
3. Work or education (e.g., whether you're having to do more work than usual)	A	B	C
4. Friends (e.g., whether you are arguing with your friends)	A	B	C
5. Rugby training (e.g., whether the effort required is hard or easy)	A	B	C
6. Climate (e.g., whether it is too hot, too cold, too dry, too wet, and so on)	A	B	C
7. Sleep (e.g., whether you are getting enough sleep)	A	B	C
8. Recreation (e.g., whether activities that you do out of sport are taking up too much time)	A	B	C
9. Health (e.g., whether you have a cold or other infections)	A	B	C
Part B: Symptoms of stress	**A = worse than normal**	**B = normal**	**C = better than normal**
1. Muscle pains (e.g., whether you have pain in your muscles)	A	B	C
2. Rugby techniques (e.g., whether your rugby technical skills are the same)	A	B	C
3. Tiredness (e.g., whether you are generally tired)	A	B	C
4. Need for rest (e.g., whether you feel that you need a rest between rugby training sessions and matches)	A	B	C
5. Supplementary work (e.g., whether you feel strong when you do your supplementary work, such as kicking, weights, or speed work)	A	B	C

INSTRUCTIONS: CONSIDER HOW YOU HAVE BEEN FEELING IN THE PREVIOUS WEEK AND CIRCLE THE APPROPRIATE RESPONSE ALONGSIDE EACH ITEM.			
Part B: Symptoms of stress	**A = worse than normal**	**B = normal**	**C = better than normal**
6. Boredom (e.g., whether you find rugby training boring)	A	B	C
7. Recovery (e.g., whether you need more time for recovery between sessions)	A	B	C
8. Irritability (e.g., whether you are irritable and things are getting on your nerves)	A	B	C
9. Weight (e.g., whether your weight is OK)	A	B	C
10. Throat (e.g., whether your throat has been sore and irritated)	A	B	C
11. Internal (e.g., whether you have been constipated or had an upset stomach)	A	B	C
12. Unexplained aches (e.g., whether you have aches or pains without evident cause)	A	B	C
13. Strength (e.g., whether you feel strong)	A	B	C
14. Enough sleep (e.g., whether you are getting enough sleep)	A	B	C
15. Between-sessions recovery (e.g., whether you are tired before rugby training starts)	A	B	C
16. General weakness (e.g., whether you feel weak all over)	A	B	C
17. Interest (e.g., whether you feel interested in rugby)		B	C
18. Arguments (e.g., whether you have been arguing with the people who are close to you)	A	B	C
19. Skin rashes (e.g., whether you have any skin rashes or irritations)	A	B	C
20. Congestion (e.g., whether your nose or sinuses are blocked)	A	B	C
21. Training effort (e.g., whether you feel able to give your best effort in rugby training)	A	B	C

(continued)

TABLE 13.2 *(continued)*

INSTRUCTIONS: CONSIDER HOW YOU HAVE BEEN FEELING IN THE PREVIOUS WEEK AND CIRCLE THE APPROPRIATE RESPONSE ALONGSIDE EACH ITEM.			
Part B: Symptoms of stress	**A = worse than normal**	**B = normal**	**C = better than normal**
22. Temper (e.g., whether you are losing your temper)	A	B	C
23. Swelling (e.g., whether lymph glands under your arms, throat, and groin are swollen)	A	B	C
24. Likeability (e.g., whether people seem to like you)	A	B	C
25. Running nose (e.g., whether your nose is running)	A	B	C

Adapted, by permission, from B.S. Rushall, 1990, "A tool for measuring stress tolerance in elite athletes," *Journal of Applied Sport Psychology* 2(1): 51-66.

Understanding Your Score

If you scored mostly A's for both sources and symptoms of stress, then you are currently going through a stressful period. If you scored lots of A's for sources of stress, then you could try to address them by speaking to appropriately trained professionals or taking action yourself. For example, if your diet is a source of stress you could create a diet plan dictating what you are going to eat and when you are going to eat it. If you are unsure, you can book an appointment with a registered dietician.

If you scored mostly A's for the symptoms of stress, you should try to address the issue of why you are experiencing these high levels of stress. You could speak to your coach about the possibility of taking a rest or altering your training to let your mind and body recover. If you continue to experience mostly A's without doing anything about it, then your performance is likely to suffer and you may experience UPS.

If you scored mostly B's for sources and symptoms of stress, then the levels of stress that you are experiencing should not have a negative effect on your rugby performance. Identify any sources and symptoms of stress that you marked as an A and try to eliminate or reduce those stressors.

If you scored mostly C's you are currently experiencing low levels of stress because you are managing the stress of training effectively. Continue doing what you are doing but monitor and take action if you start experiencing more stress.

Monitoring Affective States

Affect refers to how we are feeling. We are always feeling something. Whether we feel slightly tired or very happy, an affective tone is always present. You can measure you affective tone by marking a cross on the affective grid in figure 13.1 (Russell, Weiss, & Mendelsohn, 1989).

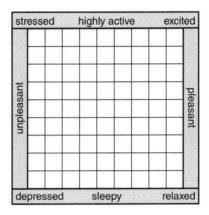

FIGURE 13.1   **Affective grid.**

From J.A. Russell, A. Weiss, and G.A. Mendelsohn, 1989, "Affect grid: A single-item scale of pleasure and arousal," *Journal of Personality and Social Psychology* 57(3): 493-502. © American Psychological Association, Inc. Adapted with permission.

You can complete this on a regular basis to monitor how you are feeling. How you feel will fluctuate depending on

- the time of day when you complete the grid,
- what you have been doing on the day that you complete the grid, and
- what you did the day before you complete the grid.

Understanding Your Affective Grid Score

If you complete this grid on a number of occasions and find that you are constantly stressed, then you need to look what is causing the stress in your life and how you can cope with it effectively. A number of solutions are presented in the chapter in this book about coping (chapter 5). But if after trying those suggestions you experience no improvements or feel depressed, you should book an appointment with your general practitioner, who will be able to help you seek further advice. If you are always sleepy when you complete the affect grid, you may know why you are feeling constantly stressed. You may be completing the affect grid too late at night or very early in the morning.

Stress and Affect Grid Results

If you have scored mostly A's on the stress questionnaire and you have reported feeling either depressed, sleepy, or tired for a month or more, then you might be experiencing overtraining. As we stated previously, no diagnostic tool is available yet, but you could consider changing your training routine and monitoring your stress levels and affect grid ratings to see whether they improve. If they do not, you could consult your general practitioner for further advice.

Summary

- Increasing your training load has the potential to cause physical stress, which may result in decreased rugby performance.
- The primary symptom of overtraining is being unable to perform to previous levels.
- Other symptoms of overtraining include unexplained aches and pains, feelings of fatigue, and sleep disturbances that occur for longer than two weeks.
- No test is currently available to diagnose overtraining.
- A number of factors appear to contribute to overtraining such as the structure and volume of training, the number of matches played, diet, sleep, and travel.
- By monitoring your stress and affect, which are both associated with overtraining, you can prevent it from happening by taking steps to reduce stress when it occurs.

14

Improving the Coach–Athlete Relationship

He knew me as well as my parents know me. He would offer help when I needed it, but just as important, he also knew when to keep quiet and give me some space. I trusted him completely because I knew he only wanted the best for me.

Tom, academy player

What Is the Coach–Athlete Relationship?

The coach–athlete relationship focuses on the relationship, alliance, or partnership between the coach and the athlete. In particular, the focus of this relationship is the thoughts, feelings, and behaviours of both the coach and the athlete (Jowett & Poczwardowski, 2007).

The relationship between the coach and his or her players is important because players who trust their coach are likely to respond to the coach's instructions more effectively (Jowett & Poczwardowski, 2007). Furthermore, the coach–athlete relationship is important for helping rugby players maximise their performance and for allowing the coach to maximise his or her ability as a coach. A positive coach–athlete relationship is also important in terms of personal growth and development of both parties (Miller & Kerr, 2002).

Callard the COACH

There is a perception out there that coaching is easy: have a plan, develop a drill for that plan, and then deliver it. Simple? Not quite! Among the many factors, the two crucial areas for me as a coach to develop are a trained "game eye" and a relationship with my players. I need to know not just the players in my main squad but all players, from the academy to first-team players.

A game eye is the ability to watch a match or practice live and make immediate adjustments without referring to a video. Coaches must be able to process information and make judgments on it. I refer to the analogy of the car journey to work. The start and the end points are the same every day, in that a match has a start and an end point, but the coach has to make lots of independent decisions along that route. No route or match is the same. A coach can have a framework but has to be adaptable within it to make the right calls for the best of the team.

Managing the relationship with your players can be extremely difficult. You will always have doubters in your squad because they are not selected, have been spoken to in the wrong way, or just feel that they are not being utilised properly.

How Is the Coach–Athlete Relationship Described?

Some argue that the coach–athlete relationship is either good or bad. Sport psychology researchers such as Jowett (2005) have explored this relationship further and have argued that the coach–athlete relationship can be placed within one of four categories:

1. **Effective and successful.** In an effective and successful coach–athlete relationship, a coach and the athlete have lots of trust, get on well, and have success in terms of rugby performance. An example of an effective and successful athlete–coach relationship would be a forwards coach who spends time coaching an aspiring hooker and develops a trust with this player, who then goes on to achieve success such as county, national, or international honours. As such, an element of mental well-being and successful performances are present.

2. **Effective and unsuccessful.** An effective and unsuccessful relationship between a coach and a player occurs when both the player and coach have emotional well-being and achieve personal growth but successful performances do not result.

3. **Ineffective and successful.** An ineffective and successful coach–athlete relationship exists when the coach has a poor working relationship with

the player, but the player performs successfully. In an ineffective coach–athlete relationship, conflict, tension, numerous disagreements, and disrespect are present from either the coach or the player, or both (Jowett & Poczwardowski, 2007).

4. Ineffective and unsuccessful. An ineffective and unsuccessful coach–athlete relationship is classified as such when the coach has a poor relationship with his or her player and performance success is absent.

Which Coach–Athlete Relationships Are Ideal?

In rank order, with 1 being the ideal coach–athlete relationship and 4 being the worst coach–athlete relationship, rank the coach–athlete relationships in table 14.1.

TABLE 14.1   Rank Order Coach-Athlete Relationship

Rank order	Coach–athlete relationship combination
1.	
2.	
3.	
4.	

From A. Nicholls and J. Callard, 2012, *Focused for rugby* (Champaign, IL: Human Kinetics).

An effective and successful coach–athlete relationship is the ideal relationship because it includes performance success and a trusting relationship between the player and the coach. You then might think that the next best athlete–coach relationship is the ineffective and successful relationship. Was that your second choice? Although this choice may be appealing, the ineffective and successful relationship and the ineffective and unsuccessful relationship would be the third and fourth placed coach–athlete relationships, respectively. Or at least they would be the least favourable relationships psychologically, because a range of negative emotions will be seen in both the coach and the player. Although the effective and unsuccessful coach–athlete relationship does not result in performance gains, the coach and player have a strong relationship and have little tension between them. Therefore, we think that the correct order should be (1) effective and successful, (2) effective and unsuccessful, (3) ineffective and successful, and (4) ineffective and unsuccessful.

Callard the COACH

The first thing I learnt from my early days as a teacher was that at no time would the entire group like me. I had to look beyond this fact and adopt an approach that would be effective for the majority of the group, for most of the time. This was my philosophy when I entered coaching, and it is my philosophy to this day. In fact, like teaching, coaching is just a custodial role. We have players for only a short time, and we want to give them the best opportunity to develop and become better players.

I think this is more applicable today, especially within professional rugby, because the movement of players from one club to another is becoming increasingly frequent. The coach has to have a constant that will help him or her remain objective with each player.

Thus, the coach should get to know the player early, be formal, and spend time discussing individual aspirations. The coach should learn about any common themes shared with the athlete and establish what desirable outcomes would look like, not just for the coach and player but also for the whole team. The coach should standardise these goals and make them tangible in training with agreed upon goals or targets. These goals should be evaluated regularly, and all of the player's involvement with the team should be based on these set goals. If no ambiguity is present about what is expected, players will likely see that they, not the coach, are central to the relationship.

Clarifying Your Experiences of the Coach–Athlete Relationship

If you are currently a coach, we would like you to think of the various relationships that you have had with players in a coaching capacity. Likewise, if you are a player, think of the various relationships that you have had with coaches in a player capacity. Either way, the idea of this exercise is to identify your experiences of various coach–athlete relationships. You might not have experienced all four types of coach–athlete relationships. The example in table 14.2 illustrates the four types of coach–athlete relationships.

Complete your own account of the coach–athlete relationship in table 14.3 on page 174. Take some time to think about the relationships you have had either as a player with different coaches or as a coach with different players.

TABLE 14.2 Coach–Athlete Relationships Example

Coach–athlete relationship type	Your experience
Effective and successful	When I was younger, one of my coaches was more than just a coach to me. I considered him a close friend. We used to chat about lots of things that happened to me at college and university. I also had a lot of success. I performed really well during the time he coached me because the advice he gave was fantastic, both technically and also life advice!
Effective and unsuccessful	When I went to university the coach we had was a top man. Everybody on the team got on really well with him because he was very easy to talk to and we all felt at ease with him. However, we did not get very good results as a team, and performances were not great. But we were all happy with the coach. It was not his fault. We were just not good enough as a team.
Ineffective and successful	I had one coach who was very arrogant and saw rugby differently from the way I do. He would want me to do one thing, but it seemed that I would always want to do everything another way. We would often argue, and I hated going to training sometimes because I knew we would argue, which would often upset me and make me feel very frustrated. I think it was the same for him, too. Even though we argued a lot and did not really get on too well, I still seemed to perform well and had a good season.
Ineffective and unsuccessful	Last season when I switched teams, I knew early on that I did not see eye to eye with the coach on anything. I thought he was arrogant and would not listen to what I said. I would often ignore his instructions and play my own way. I had some shocking performances playing for him and never got my form back.

TABLE 14.3   Coach–Athlete Relationships

Coach–athlete relationship type	Your experience
Effective and successful	
Effective and unsuccessful	
Ineffective and successful	
Ineffective and unsuccessful	

From A. Nicholls and J. Callard, 2012, *Focused for rugby* (Champaign, IL: Human Kinetics).

What Factors Determine the Coach–Athlete Relationship Type?

Jowett (2005) stated that the coach–athlete relationship is determined by the four Cs, which refer to closeness, commitment, complementarity, and co-orientation.

Closeness   An athlete could have a close relationship with a coach, in which the athlete and coach care about each other, value each other, and support each other (Hellstedt, 1987). Conversely, in an athlete–coach relationship that lacks closeness, the athlete and coach do not help each other, do not care about each other, and do not support each other.

Co-orientation   Co-orientation refers to the degree in which a coach and an athlete establish shared views within their relationship about various matters, such as rugby or life in general. The coach and athlete negotiate and discuss views of want they want to achieve (Jowett & Meek, 2000; Clark & Reiss, 1988).

Complementarity   This aspect represents how the athlete and coach behave around each other. For example, if the player adopts a caring and inquisitive outlook with his or her coach, the coach is likely to respond with similar behaviours. This dimension also includes an element of dominance and submission. Typically, the coach provides instructions and the athlete listens and implements such instructions. In certain coach–athlete relationships, however, the player may try to adopt the dominant position in the relationship in the hope that the coach will be submissive.

Commitment   Commitment relates to how devoted both the player and coach are to maintaining their relationship and thus achieving success.

Ways of Improving the Coach–Athlete Relationship: Coach's Perspective

Sport psychology researchers such as Mageau and Vallerand (2003) outlined a number of ways in which you, as the coach, can improve the coach–athlete relationship.

Give Your Player or Players Some Choice—Within Reason   Give the players whom you coach some choice but impose some limits and rules associated with such choices. For example, you might think that it is in the best interest of a player to work on both speed and a technical skill within a specific session. The player could be given the opportunity to choose which activity to do first.

Provide a Rationale   Besides giving your players some choice, give them a reason for performing each task that you ask them to perform. It might seem obvious to you why you would ask players to work on a specific task, but it might not be as clear to them.

Callard the COACH

I signed a young scrum-half from a Welsh junior club. He had outstanding core skills for that position and added greatly to our squad. We were already blessed with an exceptionally talented scrum-half who had represented his country many times. Competition for starting in the team was now going to be healthy. But the new player was becoming increasingly frustrated because of his lack of game time. He usually got off the bench, in most cases, when the game was done and dusted! All the aspirations that he had were starting to be eaten away by his lack of involvement and his frustration toward me as the coach.

It was time for a chat. Things were slipping, not alarmingly, but enough to cause concern to the team if I had left it unattended. I felt for his frustration and understood why he thought that there was a problem. He was not getting game time and thus thought that international honours would not be within his reach, because competitors were playing regularly and getting noticed. This was a big driver for him, as it had been for me. I wanted this boy to become the best player he could possibly be.

We agreed on a new set of goals and the process by which we would achieve them. I set up early morning sessions, to which we both contributed in design, although he mainly drove what he wanted to achieve from them. His competitors were there as well; thus, the players could spur each other on. The goal was individually led, but it was for the benefit of the whole squad. Blocks of matches were assigned to each player so that the player could have a run without fear of being dropped the following week. Windows of development were also pencilled in, and extra sessions were added to aid the player's development. In time his game involvement increased, and consequently his international aspirations were met.

Acknowledge Feelings Show your players that you understand how they are feeling whilst travelling to matches, during training sessions, or during matches. By showing the players that you understand what and how they are feeling, you make them feel important.

Give Players the Chance to Use Their Initiative As a coach you should allow players to use their initiative, in a supportive manner. For example, you could ask the players which areas they think they need to work on and how they would go about doing this. This discussion could determine the course of action that you are going to take.

Provide Feedback That is Informative and Noncontrolling Giving a player feedback has two primary functions: (a) it provides the player with information on a specific task, which can lead to improvement by implementing relevant feedback, and (*b*) it can also be controlling, because giving a player positive feedback encourages the player to perform the specific behaviour again (Ryan, 1982). Therefore, feedback should not have an element of control to it. The feedback "You played well today in training—keep that up and you will get selected for the next match" or "You kicked well today, just as you should every game" includes an element of the coach demonstrating control over the player. The coach could have said, "You tackled well today in training—your body position was excellent" or "Your kicking action was strong today." These statements place more emphasis on the information in the feedback, which is less controlling because there is less emphasis on consequences.

Avoid Ego-Oriented Behaviour   Do not compare your players to other players, because they will become preoccupied with other players. Instead, when you work with players, focus on improvements that they can make in their own game and how they can develop over time.

Ways of Improving the Coach–Athlete Relationship: Player's Perspective

At times the coach-athlete relationship may be poor, which could have negative effects on the well-being of the coach and the rugby player, in addition to negatively affecting performance. When the coach-athlete relationship is poor, there are a number of steps that both the player and the coach can do to improve these relations.

Acknowledge Feelings   Although your coach may be older and more experienced than you are, remember that he or she has feelings and be aware of this when communicating with him or her.

Use Nonconfrontational Questioning   If you do not agree with the decisions that your coach has made, ask questions, but in a nonconfrontational way. For example, you may be disappointed on hearing the news that you have been dropped from the team. Instead of speaking to the coach immediately, a more productive approach may be to wait at least several hours or until the next day to speak to the coach. Direct your questioning toward what you can improve to get your place back. Being disappointed is only natural if you are dropped in favour of another player.

Think About Your Behaviour   If your coach asks you to do something that you do not want to do, instead of refusing to perform the behaviour (e.g., additional kicking practice or a specific set play within a match) speak to your coach so that you can understand his or her perspective.

Conflict in the Coach–Athlete Relationship and What to Do When It Happens

Whether you are a player or a coach, you have probably experienced some conflict in the coach–athlete relationship. A number of issues might cause conflict between a coach and the player. Issues such as playing time, team tactics, training regimes, approachability of the coach, and understanding between the coach and players are factors that cause players to experience conflict with their coach. Factors such as attitude, work rate, commitment, rule breaking, and undermining team cohesion are factors that have irritated coaches and caused friction between coaches and players (LaVoi, 2004).

When conflict occurs within the coach–athlete relationship, both parties must make an effort to manage the conflict. In some instances, however, it may be impossible to eradicate the conflict between the coach and the player (LaVoi, 2007). Nevertheless, attempts should be made to resolve trouble within coach–athlete relationships. One such approach is known as conflict management. Five different approaches can be used to manage conflict (Rahim, 2002).

1. **Integrating.** Integrating involves the coach and the player having an open and honest exchange of their views, with the aim of seeking alternatives solutions to the current issues (e.g., changing training structure, making different travel arrangements, modifying the roles of players within a team, and so on).

2. **Compromising.** Both the coach and the athlete give up something and make a compromise to the situation, such as agreeing to spend more time on the training field.

3. **Obliging.** Obliging refers to attempts to minimise the differences in points of views between the coach and players through discussion.

4. **Dominating.** Domination occurs when one individual in the coach–athlete relationship forces his or her position onto the other individual. An example of this would be a coach saying, "If you do not attend training three times a week you will be dropped to the second team" or a player saying, "If I don't get picked again this season I will play for another team next season."

5. **Avoiding.** Avoiding occurs when neither the player nor the coach confronts the issues, so the conflict continues.

These examples of conflict management techniques represent steps that a coach or player can take to manage a conflict. But the right form of conflict management must be chosen for the given situation. The dominating form of conflict management has the potential to be the most destructive, because it may cause differences between the player and coach to become irreconcilable. Obliging will be unsuccessful if neither the coach nor the player is willing or able to concede that the other viewpoint is correct, but if this technique is successful it has the potential to resolve conflict. The technique most likely to be successful is the compromising technique whereby both the coach and the player are willing to back down on their viewpoints. If the coach and the athlete take the avoiding approach to conflict, then the relationship is likely to deteriorate over time. Each of the conflict management techniques has advantages and disadvantage, so caution is warranted before adopting a particular approach to conflict management. The first step should always be for the coach and the player to attempt to integrate their perspectives so that they can move forward and continue their work together.

Summary

- The coach–athlete relationship focuses on the relationship, alliance, or partnership between the coach and the athlete.
- Coach–athlete relationships fall into four categories: (1) effective and successful, (2) effective and unsuccessful, (3) ineffective and successful, and (4) ineffective and unsuccessful.
- The athlete–coach relationship is determined by the four Cs: closeness, commitment, complementarity, and co-orientation.
- The coach–athlete relationship can be improved by giving players choices (within limits, of course), providing rationale for tasks, acknowledging feelings, and providing noncontrolling feedback.
- If conflict between a coach and an athlete occurs, both parties must attempt to manage the conflict. The first step of effective conflict management is integration, whereby both parties air their views.

CHAPTER 15

Leading Effectively

He always got the best out of his players, because no one ever wanted to let him down or each other down, because the bond he built between us all was so strong. We would have done anything for him and each other.

William, ex-international player

What Is Leadership?

Leadership occurs when a person influences others to do what he or she wants them to do to achieve specific goals (Murray & Mann, 2001). Within rugby, the coach or captain of a team can influence how his or her players think or play during matches. A good leader knows how to get the best out of the players. For example, some players may respond better to being given firm instructions or to being told off after making a mistake because they use the criticism as extra motivation. Other players might go into a shell and respond negatively to firm instructions. Those players require a more caring approach from the leader. To become a better a leader, you need to be aware of the dynamics of leadership, which involve the relationships between the leader, the other players, and the situations.

Are leaders all alike? The answer to this question is no—not all leaders are alike. Research has suggested that effective leaders can have various personalities. For example, one coach or captain might be calm and an extremely successful leader, whereas an equally successful coach or captain may lose his or her temper on a regular basis. Five different leadership styles have been identified.

Leadership Styles

A leadership style refers to how the coach makes decisions and what processes are involved in making decisions. The five leadership styles are autocratic,

autocratic-consultative, consultative-individual style, consultative-group style, and group (Chelladurai & Trail, 2001).

- **Autocratic style.** Coaches or leaders who follow an autocratic style solves all problems themselves, making use of all the information that they have at the time they make the decision.

- **Autocratic-consultative style.** Leaders who follow this approach seek information from other coaches or other players whom they believe have relevant information. A decision is made independently after this consultation.

- **Consultative-individual style.** The coach speaks to all the players and other coaches individually and makes a decision, which may or may not include contribution of others.

- **Consultative-group style.** Leaders who adopt this approach speak to the group as a whole and discuss any issues or problems in front of the group. As with the consultative-individual style of leadership, the final decision made by the coach may or may not include the contribution of others.

- **Group style.** The coach presents the problems to all the players and coaches. The other players and coaches then make a joint decision without any input from the head coach.

The styles of leadership are on a continuum. At one end of the continuum the coach makes all the decisions himself or herself (i.e., autocratic style of leadership). At the other end of the continuum the coach has no input and the players make all the decisions (i.e., group style of leadership). Within sport, the autocratic and the consultative-group models of leadership are the most widely preferred leadership styles of coaches and captains. The effectiveness of the style used, however, depends on the situational circumstances (Weinberg & Gould, 2011).

Callard the PLAYER

The captain got on the bus and launched into the side: "It is a big cup game today, and we are going to hit them head on, make every tackle, front up in the aggression department, and seize every opportunity that comes our way. Stand tall, stand together, and take nothing from them. It may be their patch and their territory, but we are going to storm it as a team. It will favour us today because we are going to be united!" It was passionate, emotional, and stirring stuff, but it was flawed! At the time the captain made this speech he was injured, so he wasn't the one who was going to be sacrificing his body. Even worse, immediately after speaking he got off the bus and drove himself to the game. Leaders sacrifice everything and offer all to the cause of the team, but this one did not. This is just one practical example of how you don't want your leader to perform!

Callard the **COACH** and **PLAYER**

Some of the best leaders I have seen in the game as both a coach and a player are those who lead from the front. They are worth their place in the side and can encourage and inspire the team around them. But this is only half of the leadership role! They have also been good communicators, both with peers and with those above. They have courageous conversations with the management and are not frightened to request what is best for the team. Finally, they are good decision makers in the heat of the battle. That doesn't mean that they make all the decisions on their own, but they can feel, read, and see what is around them.

Myths About Leadership

A number of myths about leadership need to be dispelled so that you can grasp what leadership is and become a better leader yourself (Hughes, Ginnett, & Curphy, 2009).

Myth #1: Good Leadership Is All About Common Sense

Good leadership is more than just common sense because, as a leader, you are dealing with people who have independent thoughts. For example, think about whether rugby coaches and captains need to act confidently. The common sense answer is yes; of course, they need to act in a confident manner. But as a leader you have to be aware that at times you need to understand that other coaches' or players' views are important. You have to be prepared to listen, take on board what they say, and act in a humble manner. Therefore, effective leadership is more than just common sense because common sense does not take into account the feelings and thoughts of the players whom you are leading.

Myth #2: Leaders Are Born, Not Made

Some people believe that leaders are born with specific genes that allow them become leaders, which is not true. Leadership is not an innate quality that some individuals are born with but others are not. We accept that people are born with specific personality traits that are associated with leadership qualities, but having those traits does not make someone a leader. For example, a person who is an extrovert and very talkative may not necessarily be good at giving talks to a team of players, nor will the introvert necessarily be ineffective at giving speeches. For example, although an introvert could by shy and quiet, he or she may be extremely knowledgeable about the game and may offer in only a few words a message that is more effective than the points made in a long speech. The experiences that we have can also mould us as people and help us become better leaders. Therefore, everyone has the potential to be a leader.

Myth #3: Leadership Is Learned Only Through Experience

Some people believe that leadership can be learned and developed only through leading. If so, the applicability of this chapter is somewhat limited! We acknowledge the importance of experience but also think that learning about leadership can help you develop as a leader.

Can a Simple Plan Help Someone Become a More Effective Leader?

Although you can work on a number of things outlined in this chapter to become a more effective leader, the answer to this question is no. We could provide you with a list of behaviours associated with great leaders, but these would not be effective in the long term. There is not a simple recipe for becoming an effective leader because effective leadership depends on the interaction between the leader, the players, and the situation. But you can work on some skills that will help you develop as leader after you have become aware of how the players and situation interact in the leadership relationship.

Leadership–Performance Relationship

Chelladurai (1990) suggested that a relationship exists between optimal team performance or team satisfaction and the behaviour of a leader. This relationship depends on the situation that the leader's behaviour occurs in (see figure 15.1).

Optimal team performance occurs only when a leader's behaviour in a certain situation matches how the players within a group would want their leader to behave (preferred leader behaviour). In particular circumstances, however, the situation may require a leader to behave in a specific manner. That is, pressure from the organisation in which the leader operates may require the leader to behave in a certain way. For example, if a player commits an offence away from rugby, the bosses of the rugby club may instruct the coach to drop the player. The coach may have no choice but to comply.

To maximise team performance, a leader must take into account the specific situation that he or she is in and the preferred leader behaviours from the players

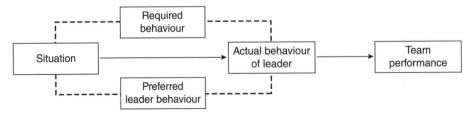

FIGURE 15.1   **The leadership–performance relationship.**

Adapted, by permission, from P. Chelladurai, 1990, "Leadership in sports: A review," *International Journal of Sport Psychology* 21(4): 328-354.

within the squad before initiating actual behaviours. Remember that as the situation changes so might the preferred leader behaviours and required behaviours. The relationship between these variables can change from situation to situation, so one form of behaviour will not be effective in all situations.

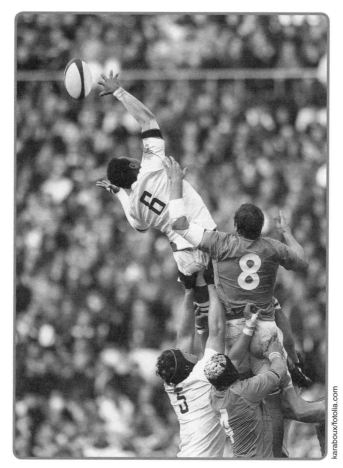

karaboux/fotolia.com

All rugby teams need leaders, players that rise above the scrum and set examples for others to follow.

Callard the COACH

A method that works well is to have a small group of players within the team form a leadership unit. This unit meets with the coach, talks out decisions, and establishes the chain of communication. For example, the group might include a defensive captain whose responsibility is to control the defensive structure and be the focal point for it. A person who has control of the lineout would be responsible for calling the options both to win the ball and to steal the ball on the opposition throw. There are no set rules about this group, but it helps to establish on-field leaders and spread the burden of responsibility. After all, the game is about the players.

Three-Skill Approach to Developing Leadership

Effective leaders have three basic skills: technical, interpersonal, and conceptual (Katz, 1955; Northouse, 2007). These skills are not personality traits because we are not born with them, but we can all learn them and use them to become better leaders.

- **Technical Skill.** Technical skills refer to your knowledge about the game of rugby such as your knowledge about attacking and defensive formations and your knowledge about specific skills such as passing technique, kicking technique, and lineout throwing.

- **Interpersonal Skill.** Interpersonal skills refer to your ability to work with other people within the team environment such as the players, other coaches, medical staff, and conditioning staff. You need to be able to communicate with people, be aware of your own perspective on various matters, and at the same time be aware of the opinions of others. Interpersonal skill is about your ability to create an atmosphere of trust whereby your players feel comfortable and secure in playing rugby and in expressing their opinions.

- **Conceptual Skill.** Conceptual skills refer to your ability to work with various ideas and concepts and then implement such concepts on the pitch. For example, a coach may develop new strategies in relation to playing a particular team. An effective leader is comfortable in presenting his or her ideas.

Callard the COACH

When the players play they should all be leaders; that is, each player is responsible for his or her particular area of the game, and all have to be accountable for their actions. As a coach I want leadership from all players, because each has to ignite and inspire the team at crucial times. One person cannot do that alone; it has to be a collective effort.

Rate Your Leadership Skills

You can assess your leadership skills by completing the questionnaire presented in table 15.1, which we adapted to rugby based on the original questionnaire produced by Northouse (2007).

Questionnaire instructions: Read each question carefully and describe how accurately the questionnaire describes you as person. Indicate your response by circling the appropriate number.

1 = not true

2 = seldom true

3 = occasionally true

4 = somewhat true

5 = very true

TABLE 15.1 Leadership Questionnaire

1	I enjoy getting into the technical detail of how different rugby skills are produced.	1	2	3	4	5
2	As a rule, adapting my ideas to people's needs is easy for me to do.	1	2	3	4	5
3	I enjoy working with abstract ideas of tactics and ways of playing different opponents.	1	2	3	4	5
4	Technical aspects of rugby fascinate me.	1	2	3	4	5
5	Being able to understand others is the most important part of my work.	1	2	3	4	5
6	Seeing the big picture comes easy to me.	1	2	3	4	5
7	One of my strengths is identifying how movements make up different skills.	1	2	3	4	5
8	One of my main concerns is to have a supportive communication climate.	1	2	3	4	5
9	I am intrigued by thinking about different ways of setting my team up to play our opponents.	1	2	3	4	5
10	Following directions comes easy to me.	1	2	3	4	5
11	Understanding the social relationships of the squad is important to me.	1	2	3	4	5
12	I enjoy working out strategies so my team can develop.	1	2	3	4	5
13	I am good at completing the tasks I am asked to do.	1	2	3	4	5
14	Getting all of the players and other coaches working together is a challenge I enjoy.	1	2	3	4	5
15	Creating team goals is rewarding.	1	2	3	4	5
16	I understand how to do the tasks required of me.	1	2	3	4	5
17	I think about how my decisions affect the players and other coaches.	1	2	3	4	5
18	Thinking about my team values and philosophy appeals to me.	1	2	3	4	5

Adapted, by permission, from P.G. Northouse, 2007, Leadership: Theory and practice, 4th ed. (Thousand Oaks, CA: SAGE Publications), 65. Permission conveyed through Copyright Clearance Center, Inc.

Scoring Your Results

The questionnaire that you have just completed is designed to measure three types of skills associated with effective leadership: technical, human, and conceptual. Score your technical skills by adding up your score for questions 1, 4, 7, 10, 13, and 16. Sum your total score for questions 2, 5, 8, 11, 14, and 17 for your total score for interpersonal skills. Finally, add up your scores for questions 3, 6, 9, 12, 15, and 18 to reveal your conceptual score. Enter these scores here:

Technical skill score: _____

Interpersonal skill score: _____

Conceptual skill score: _____

Interpreting Your Score

The scores that you received for technical skills, interpersonal skills, and conceptual skills are out of a maximum of 25. By looking at the scores and noting the differences among them, you can determine your strengths and weaknesses. You will also be able to identify areas in which you can improve. For example, if your score is lower than you would like for either technical or conceptual skills, you can increase your knowledge on those areas by reading coaching manuals or attending coaching conferences. Alternatively, if your interpersonal skill is somewhat lower than you would like, you can work on developing your interpersonal skills and the way in which you interact with your players and other coaches.

What Interpersonal Skills Are Associated With Being an Effective Leader?

Bill Parcels, a successful coach who won two Super Bowls in American football, identified a number of skills that he believed were crucial to successful leadership. Most of the skills can be classified as interpersonal skills because they are related to the way in which a leader communicates with others and his or her values toward other people (Parcells & Coplon, 1995). The meaning of each leadership skill is presented in table 15.2.

TABLE 15.2 Skills and Meanings Associated With Effective Leadership

Skill	Meaning
Integrity	Integrity means being honest and truthful with your players at all times. Integrity also refers to behaving in a way that reflects your values, principles, and beliefs. Therefore, when leading, your leadership should reflect your values and beliefs even in the face of pressure from players and other people within a club.
Flexibility	You need to be flexible in your methods and the way in which you treat people. For example, you can take into account personal circumstances of your players when making decisions.
Loyalty	You must have loyalty within the team that you lead. Loyalty is one of the most important factors in team success. You can promote loyalty by being loyal to all your players and encouraging them to do the same with you as the coach and their fellow players.
Confidence	You should empower other coaches and players with confidence. You can do this by giving other staff members and players additional responsibility and decision-making opportunities. Support them in their efforts to make decisions.
Accountability	All teams, including the leader, have to be accountable for everything that they do. Therefore, you should promote a culture in which individuals within the team take responsibility for their decisions and actions.
Candor	Candor refers to being open and honest, but it is not enough to be open and honest when relaying messages to players. Parcells suggested that you have to consider what the players are able to take in when you give them a message. For instance, if you give a player instruction during a match he or she might take in less information, which will diminish the effect of the message. Consider what you say to a player as well as when you say it.
Patience	You must be patient, especially when you lead a team that struggles with performances. Patience is important because as a leader you need to know not only how to implement changes but also when to implement changes.

Six Steps to Becoming a More Effective Leader

Lawson (2009) proposed six steps to becoming an effective leader. At the start of this chapter we stated that there are no quick fixes to becoming a more effective leader. Likewise, these six steps will take an initial effort and require continuous effort over time. These six steps can become a way of leadership that you do every day to lead your players.

Step 1: Clarifying Your Centre The centre refers to your inner beliefs and core values. When your inner beliefs and core values are clear—that is, you know exactly what you stand for—you are more likely to have a positive and powerful influence on players. According to Lawson (2009) some people never test their inner beliefs and therefore never become leaders. When you are a leader, your inner beliefs are always questioned. To clarify your centre or to identify your inner beliefs, you have to understand what engages you. Leadership is the act of engaging yourself because when you become engaged you can influence others, without even trying. To identify what engages you, answer the questions in table 15.3.

TABLE 15.3 Clarifying Your Center

Question	Answer
What captures your imagination?	
What are your dreams?	
What is that causes you to smile, increases your pulse, and causes you to speak animatedly with other players or coaches?	
What is it that motivates you to expend your physical and mental energy in rugby?	

From A. Nicholls and J. Callard, 2012, *Focused for rugby* (Champaign, IL: Human Kinetics).

By answering these questions you are identifying what engages you and what your inner beliefs are, which is referred to as clarifying your centre. Completing this procedure is not a task that you do only once; it is a lifelong task because your beliefs can change with age and experience. Being aware of any changes that occur is crucial.

Step 2: Clarifying What Is Possible   In step 1 you look inward to identify your inner beliefs, whereas in step 2 you determine what is possible and look outward. Essentially, you have to work out where you want to take your team and what you want to achieve. Be realistic when identifying what is possible for your team to achieve within the time that you have available.

Step 3: Clarifying What Others Can Contribute   You must be able to clarify what players and coaches can do because without a firm understanding of how they will contribute to your vision for the team, they are not likely to commit to the cause. You should not underestimate the importance of being able to judge others' capabilities, because this skill is crucial to being an effective leader. For example, you might ask questions such as these: Which players have the skills to play the way that you want the team to play? Which players have the attitude to train the way that you want them to train? Which players have the potential to develop new skills? Are all the players currently playing in their best positions? By asking these questions and other questions to clarify what your players can do, you are starting to assess how your players and coaching staff will help you to achieve your goals.

Step 4: Supporting Others So That They Can Contribute   As a leader you should support your players and coaches by encouraging and developing them as people and players. You can do this by empowering your coaches and players to take responsibility and by identifying ways in which your players can become better. Encourage your players to be the best they can be and do not punish mistakes, especially if they make mistakes when they were attempting to play in the manner that you want. Be constructive in any criticism that you give players so that they can go away and work on aspects of their game.

Step 5: Being Relentless   After you have established the vision for your team, be relentless in achieving it. You can do this by not letting setbacks discourage you as they occur along the way and by directing enormous stamina and energy toward achieving success.

Step 6: Measuring and Celebrating Progress   Most players or coaches who work under you require positive feedback at some point to give them motivation and reassurance that they are doing the right things. Statements such as "You are improving your tackling" and "You are really grasping how I want you to play, which is excellent" will encourage your players. The most effective leaders realise the importance of encouraging their players.

Summary

- Leadership occurs when a person influences others to do what he or she wants them to do.
- Leaders are not all alike, and leaders have various styles. There is no right or wrong approach to leadership.
- Effective leaders have technical skills, interpersonal skills, and conceptual skills.
- How you behave as a leader should be influenced by the situation because circumstances will affect the success of your decisions.
- You can become a more effective leader by adhering to the six steps of effective leadership.

References

Chapter 1

Burton, D., & Naylor, S. (2002). The Jekyll/Hyde nature of goals: Revisiting and updating goal setting in sport. In T. Horn (Ed.), *Advances in sport psychology* (pp. 459–499). Champaign, IL: Human Kinetics.

Jordan, M. (1994). *I can't accept not trying*. San Francisco: Harper.

Locke, E.A., & Latham, G.P. (1990). *A theory of goal setting and task performance*. Englewood Cliffs, NJ: Prentice Hall.

Chapter 2

Dale, G.A., & Wrisberg, C.A. (1996). The use of a performance profiling technique in a team setting: Getting the athletes and the coach on the "same page." *Sport Psychologist, 10,* 261–277.

Jones, G. (1993). The role of performance profiling in cognitive behavioral interventions in sport. *Sport Psychologist, 7,* 160–172.

Chapter 4

Clough, P., Earle, K., & Sewell, D. (2002). Mental toughness: The concept and its measurement. In I. Cockerill (Ed.), *Solutions in Sport Psychology* (pp. 32–45). London, Thomson.

Jones, G., Hanton, S., & Connaughton, D. (2007). A framework of mental toughness in the world's best performers. *Sport Psychologist, 21,* 243–264.

Nicholls, A.R., Polman, R.C.J., Levy, A., & Backhouse, S.H. (2008). Mental toughness, optimism, and coping among athletes. *Personality and Individual Differences, 44,* 1182–92.

Seligman, M. (1998). *Learned optimism: How to change your mind and your life*. New York: Free Press.

Chapter 5

Folkman, S. (1991). Coping across the life span: Theoretical issues. In E.M. Cummings, A.L. Greene, & K.H. Karraker (Eds.) *Life-span developmental psychology: Perspectives on stress and coping* (pp. 3–19). Hillsdale, NJ: Erlbaum.

Haney, C.J., & Long, B.C. (1995). Coping effectiveness: A path analysis of self-efficacy, control, coping, and performance in sport competitions. *Journal of Applied Social Psychology, 25,* 1726–1746.

Jordan, M. (1994). *I can't accept not trying*. San Francisco: Harper.

Lazarus, R.S. (1999). *Stress and emotion: A new synthesis*. New York: Springer.

Nicholls, A.R., Levy, A.R., Jones, L., Rengamani, M., & Polman, R.C.J. (in press). An exploration of the two-factor schematization of relational meaning and emotions among professional rugby union players. *International Journal of Sport and Exercise Psychology*.

Chapter 6

Hall, C.R., & Martin, K.A. (1997). Measuring movement imagery abilities: A revision of the Movement Imagery Questionnaire. *Journal of Mental Imagery, 21*, 143–154.

Hale, B. D., & Whitehouse, A. (1998). The effects of imagery manipulated appraisal on intensity and direction of competition anxiety. *The Sport Psychologist*, 12, 40-51.

Harris, D. V., & Robinson, W. J. (1986). The effects of skill level on EMG activity during internal and external imagery. *Journal of Sport Psychology,* 8, 105-111.

Kosslyn, S. M., Ganis, G., & Thompson, W. L. (2001). Neural foundations of imagery. *Nature Reviews Neuroscience,* 2, 635-739.

Murphy, S., Nordin, S., & Cumming, J. (2008). Imagery in sport, exercise,and dance. In. T. Horn (Ed.), *Advances in sport psychology* (3rd ed., pp. 297-324). Champaign, IL: Human Kinetics.

Weinberg, R., & Gould, D. (2011). Foundations of sport and exercise psychology. Champaign, IL: Human Kinetics.

Chapter 7

Weinberg, R., & Gould, D. (2011). Foundations of sport and exercise psychology. Champaign, IL: Human Kinetics.

Chapter 8

Baumeister, R.F. (1984). Choking under pressure: Self-consciousness and paradoxical effects of incentives on skilful performance. *Journal of Personality and Social Psychology*, *46*, 610–620.

Beilock, S.L., & Carr, T.H. (2001). On the fragility of skilled performance: What governs choking under pressure? *Journal of Experimental Psychology: General*, *130*, 701–725.

Beilock, S.L., & Gray, R. (2007). Why do athletes choke under pressure? In G. Tenenbaum & R.C. Eklund (Eds.), *Handbook of sport psychology* (3rd ed., pp. 425–444). Hoboken, NJ: Wiley.

Freud, S. (1922). *Introductory lectures on psychoanalysis.* London: George Allen & Unwin.

Jordett, G. (2010). Choking under pressure as self-destructive behavior. In A.R. Nicholls (Ed), *Coping in sport: Theory, methods, and related constructs* (pp. 239–259). New York: Nova Science.

Leary, M.R. (2004). *The curse of the self: Self-awareness, egotism, and the quality of human life*. New York: Oxford University Press.

Lonsdale, C., & Tam, J.T.M. (2008). On the temporal and behavioural consistency of pre-performance routines: An intra-individual analysis of elite basketball players' free throw shooting accuracy. *Journal of Sports Sciences*, *26*, 259–266.

Mesagno, C., Marchant, D., & Morris, T. (2008). A pre-performance routine to alleviate choking in "choking-susceptible" athletes. *Sport Psychologist*, *22*, 439–457.

Nicholls, A.R., Levy, A.R., Jones, L., Rengamani, M., & Polman, R.C.J. (2011). An exploration of the two-factor schematization of relational meaning and emotions among professional rugby union players. *International Journal of Sport and Exercise Psychology*, *9*, 78-91.

Nideffer, R.M. (1992). *Psyched to win*. Champaign, IL: Leisure Press.

Chapter 9

Jackson, S.A. (1995). Factors influencing the occurrence of flow in elite athletes. *Journal of Applied Sport Psychology, 7,* 138–166.

Jackson, S.A., & Csikszentmihalyi, M. (1999). *Flow in sports.* Champaign, IL: Human Kinetics.

Russell, W.D. (2001). An examination of flow states occurrence in college athletes. *Journal of Sport Behaviour, 24,* 83–107.

Chapter 10

Arnett, C. E. (1987). *The relationship of marital partnership status to husband/wife bargaining mode:* Dissertation Abstracts International.

Faupel, A., Herrick, E., & Sharp, P. (1998). *Anger management: A practical guide.* London: David Fulton.

Harbin, T.J. (2000). *Beyond anger: A guide for men.* Cambridge, MA: Da Capo Press.

Hymans, M. (2009). *Whole-school strategies for anger management: Practical materials for senior managers, teachers, and support staff.* London: Optimus Education.

Chapter 11

Blakeslee, T.R. (1980). *The right brain.* New York: Anchor Press.

Carson, F., & Polman, R.C.J. (2010). The facilitative nature of avoidance coping within sports injury rehabilitation. *Scandinavian Journal of Medicine and Science in Sports, 20,* 235–240.

Durso-Cupal, D.D. (1996). The efficacy of guided imagery for recovery from anterior cruciate ligament (ACL) replacement. *Journal of Applied Sport Psychology, 8*(Suppl.), S56.

Heil, J. (1993). *Psychology of sport injury.* Champaign, IL: Human Kinetics.

Kerr, H.A., Curtis, C., Micheli, L.J., Kocher, M.S., Zurakowski, D., Kemp, S.P.T., & Brooks, J.H.M. (2008). Collegiate rugby union injury patterns in New England: A prospective cohort study. *British Journal of Sports Medicine, 42,* 595–603.

Kindermann, W. (1988). Metabolic and hormonal reactions in overtraining. *Seminars in Orthopaedics, 3,* 207–216.

Nicholls, A.R., Levy, A.R., Jones, L., Rengamani, M., & Polman, R.C.J. (2011). An exploration of the two-factor schematization of relational meaning and emotions among professional rugby union players. *International Journal of Sport and Exercise Psychology, 9,* 78-91.

Smith, R.E., Ptacek, J.T., & Patterson, E. (2000). Moderator effects of cognitive and somatic trait anxiety on the relation between life stress and physical injuries. *Anxiety, Stress, and Coping, 13,* 269–288.

Taylor, J., & Taylor, S. (1997). *Psychological approaches to sports injury rehabilitation.* NY: Aspen.

Udry, E. (1997). Coping and social support among injured athletes following surgery. *Journal of Sport & Exercise Psychology, 19,* 71–90.

Williams, J.M., & Andersen, M.B. (1998). Psychological antecedents of sport and injury: Review and critique of the stress and injury model. *Journal of Sport and Exercise Psychology, 10,* 5–25.

Williams, J.M., Tonyman, P., & Andersen, M.B. (1991). The effects of stressors and coping resources on anxiety and peripheral narrowing. *Journal of Applied Sport Psychology, 3,* 126–141.

Chapter 12

Williams, J.M., & Harris, D.V. (2001). Relaxation techniques and energizing techniques for regulation arousal. In J.M. Williams (Ed.), *Applied sport psychology: Personal growth to peak performance* (pp. 229–246). Mountain View, CA: Mayfield.

Chapter 13

Armstrong, L.E., & VanHeest, J.L. (2002). The unknown mechanism of the overtraining syndrome: Clues from depression and psychoneuroimmunology. *Sports Medicine, 32*, 185–209.

Halson, S.L., & Jeukendrup, A.E. (2004). Does overtraining exist? An analysis of overreaching and overtraining research. *Sports Medicine, 14*, 967–981.

Kreider, R.B., Fry, A.C., & O'Toole, M.L. (1998). Overtraining in sport: Terms, definitions, and prevalence. In R.B. Kreider, A.C. Fry, & M.L. O'Toole (Eds.), *Overtraining in sport* (pp. vii–ix). Champaign, IL: Human Kinetics.

Kuipers, H. (1998). Training and overtraining: An introduction. *Medicine and Science in Sport and Exercise, 30*, 1137–1139.

Nicholls, A.R., McKenna, J., Backhouse, S.H., & Polman, R.C.J. (in press). The perceived risk factors associated with symptoms of overtraining among professional rugby union players. *International Journal of Sport and Exercise Psychology.*

Polman, R.C.J., & Houlan, K. (2004). A Cumulative stress and training continuum model: A multidisciplinary approach to unexplained underperformance syndrome. *Research in Sports Medicine, 12*, 301–316.

Richardson, S.O., Andersen, M.B., & Morris, T. (2008). *Overtraining athletes: Personal journeys in sport*. Champaign, IL: Human Kinetics.

Rushall, B.R. (1990). A tool for measuring stress tolerance in elite athletes. *Journal of Applied Sport Psychology, 2*, 51–66.

Russell, J.A., Weiss, A., & Mendelsohn, G.A. (1989). Affect grid: A single-item scale of pleasure and arousal. *Journal of Personality and Social Psychology, 57*, 493–502.

Chapter 14

Clark, M.S., & Reiss, H.T. (1988). Interpersonal processes in close relationships. *Annual Review of Psychology, 39*, 609–672.

Hellstedt, J.C. (1987). The coach/parent/athlete relationship. *Sport Psychologist, 1*, 151–160.

Jowett, S. (2005). On enhancing and repairing the coach–athlete relationship. In S. Jowett & M. Jones (Eds.), *The psychology of coaching* (pp. 14–26). Leicester: British Psychological Society.

Jowett, S., & Meek, G.A. (2000). Coach–athlete relationships in married couples: An exploratory content analysis. *Sport Psychologist, 14*, 157–175.

Jowett, S., & Poczwardowski, A. (2007). Understanding the coach–athlete relationship. In S. Jowett & D. Lavallee (Eds.), *Social Psychology in sport* (pp. 3–14). Champaign, IL: Human Kinetics.

LaVoi, N.M. (2004). Dimensions of closeness and conflict in the coach–athlete relationship. Paper presented at the meeting of the Association for the Advancement of Applied Sport Psychology, Minneapolis, MN.

LaVoi, N.M. (2007). Expanding the interpersonal dimension: Closeness in the coach–athlete relationship. *International Journal of Sport Science and Coaching, 4*, 497–512.

Mageau, G.A., & Vallerand, R.J. (2003). The coach–athlete relationship: A motivational model. *Journal of Sports Sciences*, *21*, 883–904.

Miller, P.S., & Kerr, G.A. (2002). Conceptualizing excellence: Past, present, and future. *Journal of Applied Sport Psychology*, *14*, 140–153.

Rahim, M. (2002). Toward a theory of managing organizational conflict. *International Journal of Conflict Management*, *13*, 206–235.

Ryan, R.M. (1982). Control and information in the intrapersonal sphere: An extension of cognitive evaluation theory. *Journal of Personality and Social Psychology*, *43*, 450–461.

Chapter 15

Chelladurai, P. (1990). Leadership in sports: A review. *International Journal of Sport Psychology*, *21*, 328–354.

Chelladurai, P., & Trail, G. (2001). Styles of decision-making in coaching. In J.M. Williams (Ed.), *Applied sport psychology: Personal growth to peak performance* (pp. 107–119). Mountain View, CA: Mayfield.

Hughes, R.L., Ginnett, R.C., & Curphy, G.C. (2009). *Leadership: Enhancing the lessons of experience*. Maidenhead, Berkshire: McGraw-Hill.

Katz, R.L. (1955). Skills of an effective administrator. *Harvard Business Review*, *33*, 33–42.

Lawson, J.G. (2009). *Level three leadership: Getting below the surface*. New Jersey: Prentice Hall.

Murray, M.C., & Mann, B.L. (2001). Effective leadership. In J.M. Williams (Ed.), *Applied sport psychology: Personal growth to peak performance* (pp. 82–106). Mountain View, CA: Mayfield.

Northouse, P.G. (2007). *Leadership: Theory and practice*. Thousand Oaks, CA: Sage.

Parcells, B., & Coplon, J. (1995). *Finding a way to win: The principles of leadership, teamwork, and motivation*. New York: Doubleday.

Weinberg, R., & Gould, D. (2011). Foundations of sport and exercise psychology. Champaign, IL: Human Kinetics.

About the Authors

Dr. Adam Nicholls, C. Psychol, AFBPsS is an Associate Fellow of the British Psychological Society and a Registered Sport and Exercise Psychologist with the Health Professions Council. He has been providing psychological support to professional rugby players for several years. Additionally, Adam has published over 40 scientific papers in international journals on topics such as coping, mental toughness, and injury rehabilitation. He has also edited a book on coping in sport. Many international rugby union players—including those who have represented the British and Irish Lions, the New Zealand All Blacks, England, Wales, Ireland, Scotland, Fiji, and Hong Kong—have participated in Adam's research, which gives him a unique insight into the psychology of participating in rugby at the highest level, which he shares with other players to help them be the best they can. Adam has the skills and experience to teach rugby players and coaches the most up-to-date psychological techniques.

Jon Callard landed four penalty goals that helped England beat New Zealand 15-9 at Twickenham in 1993 on his test debut. Five years later he scored all of Bath's points in the 19-18 win over Brive, which earned Bath the accolade of being the first English club to lift the Heineken Cup. Jon's coaching career dates back to 1998, when he was appointed assistant to the assistant coach at Bath, and then became head coach two years later. After that he had a spell as Leeds Carnegie's first team coach in 2002. Jon is a former physical education and science teacher at Downside, and played six times for the Barbarians from 1994 to 1997 and as a specialist fullback for Bath. His 2,087 points from 210 matches contributed hugely to Bath's triumphs, including four Twickenham cup final victories and five Courage League titles between 1990 and 1996.